CIVIL RIGHTS DECISIONS
OF THE UNITED STATES
SUPREME COURT
THE 20th CENTURY

MAUREEN HARRISON & STEVE GILBERT
EDITORS

CIVIL RIGHTS DECISIONS SERIES

EXCELLENT BOOKS
SAN DIEGO, CALIFORNIA

EXCELLENT BOOKS
Post Office Box 927105
San Diego, CA 92192-7105

Publisher's Cataloging in Publication Data

Civil Rights Decisions Of The United States Supreme Court: The 20th Century/
Maureen Harrison, Steve Gilbert, editors.
p. cm. - (Civil Rights Decisions Series)
Bibliography: p.
Includes Index.
1. Civil Rights - United States - Cases, 2. United States. Supreme Court.
I. Title. II. Harrison, Maureen. III. Gilbert, Steve.
IV. Series: Civil Rights Decisions.
KF4748 H24 1994   LC 93-74635
342.'73-dc20
ISBN 1-880780-05-4

INTRODUCTION

In what I have done I cannot claim to have acted from any peculiar consideration of the colored people as a separate and distinct class in the community, but from the simple conviction that all the individuals of that class are members of the community, and, in virtue of their manhood, entitled to every original right enjoyed by any other member. We feel, therefore, that all legal distinctions between individuals of the same community, founded in any such circumstances as color, origin, and the like, are hostile to the genius of our institutions, and incompatible with the true history of American liberty.

Abraham Lincoln

This book, the second in the Civil Rights Decisions Series, is based on what Abraham Lincoln called "original rights" - what we now call civil rights. Lincoln held the conviction that all members of the American community, regardless of color or origin, were entitled to every civil right enjoyed by any other member. The United States Supreme Court has not always shared this conviction. In 1857 a pre-Civil War Court held, in the case of *Dred Scott v. Sanford,* that human slavery, a total denial of civil rights, was legal. Speaking for the *Scott* Court Chief Justice Taney wrote: [T]hat unfortunate race . . . had for more than a century before been regarded as beings of an inferior order, and altogether unfit to associate with the white race . . . so far inferior, that that had no rights which the white man was bound to respect." Again, in 1896, a post-Civil War Court held, in the case of *Plessy v. Ferguson,* that racial segregation, another total denial of civil rights, was equally legal. Speaking for the *Plessy* Court, Justice Henry Brown wrote: "If the civil and political rights of both races be equal, one cannot be inferior to the other civilly or politically. If one race be inferior to the other socially, the Constitution of the United States cannot put them upon the same plane."

In **Civil Rights Decisions: The 20th Century**, we have selected what we consider to be the Supreme Court's most important civil rights decisions issued from the turn of the century through the present day. This second volume of the Civil Rights Decisions Series is divided into two sections: **The Japanese American Decisions** and **The African American Decisions**. In each section we have selected for their legal and historic significance the Court's civil rights decisions that best represent the story of twentieth century America's treatment of these two, and by extension all, racial minorities.

THE JAPANESE AMERICAN DECISIONS

December 7, 1941 was not America's only day of infamy during the Second World War. Tens of thousands of loyal Japanese Americans lost their civil rights to racial prejudice and the hysteria of war. General John DeWitt, in charge of the evacuation of the Japanese Americans from the West Coast, wrote: "The Japanese race is an enemy race and, while many second and third generation Japanese born on United States soil, possessed of United States citizenship, have became "Americanized," the racial strains are undiluted. . . . There are indications that these [Japanese Americans] are organized and ready for concerted action at a favorable opportunity. The very fact that no sabotage has taken place to date is a disturbing and confirming indication that such action will be taken."

Hirabayashi v. United States, The Japanese American Curfew Case, and *Korematsu v. United States*, The Japanese American Concentration Camp Case, serve to illustrate the fragility of minority civil rights in times of crisis. Chief Justice Warren wrote 30 years later: "I have since deeply regretted the removal order and my own testimony advocating it. . . . It was not in keeping with our American concept of freedom and the rights of citizens."

THE AFRICAN AMERICAN DECISIONS

Dr. Martin Luther King, Jr. wrote of civil rights decisions: "Life is breathed into a judicial decision by the persistent exercise of legal rights until they become usual and ordinary in human experience." The African American Decisions are divided into eight sections, comprising thirteen individual Supreme Court cases spanning fifty-five years. The persistent exercise of the civil rights won in these cases have made them usual and ordinary in everyday experience. Included are civil rights decisions on:

MOB JUSTICE
The Arkansas Murder Trial of the Elaine Nine
The Georgia Rape Trial of the Scottsboro Boys

SCHOOL DESEGREGATION
Brown v. Board of Education I & II
The Little Rock Desegregation Crisis
Court Ordered Busing

PUBLIC TRANSPORTATION
The Woman Who Would Not Go To The Back Of the Bus

THE RIGHT TO VOTE
The Texas Election Cases

RACIALLY RESTRICTED HOUSING
The Keep Out Of Our Neighborhood Case

PUBLIC ACCOMMODATIONS
No Room At The Heart Of Atlanta Motel Case

INTERRACIAL MARRIAGE
The Love Knows No Color Case

AFFIRMATIVE ACTION
University of California v. Bakke

The United States Supreme Court is the Court of Last Appeal in all cases concerning Constitutional rights and protections. The Justices of the Court, appointed by the President and approved by the Congress, have decided many famous and and equally infamous constitutional cases dealing with the civil rights of Native, African, and Asian Americans. The selected Civil Rights Decisions presented in this book are carefully edited versions of the official texts issued by the Supreme Court in *United States Reports*. Judge Learned Hand wrote: "The language of the law must not be foreign to the ears of those who are to obey it." We, as editors, have made every effort to make the the language of these decisions less "foreign." We have attempted to replace esoteric legalese with plain English without damaging the original decisions. Edited out are long alpha-numeric legal citation and wordy wrangles over abstract points of procedure. Edited in are definitions (writ of habeas corpus = an order from a judge to bring a person to court), translations (certiorari = the decision of the Court to review a case), identifications (Appellant = Dred Scott, Appellee = John Sandford), and explanations (who the parties were, who the members of the Court were, what laws were at issue, what constitutional provisions were involved, where the case originated, how the case reached the court, and what the final decision was).

You will find in this book the opinion of the Court as expressed by the Justice chosen to speak for the majority. Preceding each edited decision we provide a brief history of the case, we note where the complete unedited decision can be found, and we give the members of the Court deciding the case. The bibliography provides a selected list of further reading on the cases and the Court. Also included for the reader's reference is a complete copy of the United States Constitution, to which every decision refers.

Supreme Court Justice Oliver Wendell Holmes, Jr. wrote in *The Common Law*: "In order to know what the law is, we must know what it has been." We hope that these two volumes of **Civil Rights Decisions,** published in the fortieth anniversary year of *Brown v. Board of Education,* and only two years shy of the hundreth anniversary of *Plessy v. Ferguson,* will let you know, in Justice Holmes' phrase, "what the law has been."

M.H. & S.G.

This book is dedicated to three
civil rights workers

James Chaney
Andrew Goodman
Michael Schwerner

murdered

June 21, 1964
Meridian, Mississippi

TABLE OF CONTENTS

THE JAPANESE AMERICAN DECISIONS

THE WORLD WAR II INTERNMENT OF JAPANESE AMERICANS

The adoption by Government, in crisis of war and of threatened invasion, of measures for the public safety, based upon the recognition of facts and circumstances which indicate that a group of one national extraction may menace that safety more than others, is not wholly beyond the limits of the Constitution.

Chief Justice Harlan Fiske Stone (1943)

It is said that we are dealing here with the case of imprisonment of a citizen in a concentration camp solely because of his [Japanese] ancestry. . . . [A]ll legal restrictions which curtail the civil rights of a single racial group are immediately suspect. That is not to say that all such restrictions are unconstitutional. It is to say that courts must subject them to the most ridged scrutiny. Pressing public necessity may sometimes justify the existence of such restrictions; racial antagonism never can.

Justice Hugo Black (1944)

THE AFRICAN AMERICAN DECISIONS

MOB JUSTICE

The Arkansas Murder Trial Case

Moore v. Dempsey
37

The trial lasted about three-quarters of an hour and in less than five minutes the jury brought in a verdict of guilty. There was never a chance for [acquittal]; if any prisoner had been acquitted . . . he could not have escaped the mob.
Justice Oliver Wendell Holmes, Jr. (1923)

The Georgia Rape Trial Case

The Scottsboro Boys
45

[A] defendant, charged with a serious crime, must not be stripped of his right to have sufficient time to advise with counsel and prepare his defense. To do that is . . . to go forward with the haste of the mob.
Justice George Sutherland (1932)

SCHOOL DESEGREGATION

Segregated Schools Are Not Equal

Brown v. Board of Education I
61

We conclude that in the field of public education the doctrine of "separate but equal" has no place. Separate educational facilities are inherently unequal. Therefore, we hold that [minors of the Negro race] are, by reason of the segregation complained of, deprived of the equal protection of the laws guaranteed by the Fourteenth Amendment.
Chief Justice Earl Warren (1954)

With All Deliberate Speed

Brown v. Board of Education II
71

The judgments below . . . are accordingly reversed and the cases are remanded to the District Courts to take such proceedings and enter such orders and decrees consistent with this opinion as are necessary and proper to admit to public schools on a racially nondiscriminatory basis with all deliberate speed the parties to these cases.

Chief Justice Earl Warren (1955)

The Little Rock Desegregation Crisis

Cooper v. Aaron
77

The Constitution created a government dedicated to equal justice under law. The Fourteenth Amendment embodied and emphasized that ideal. State support of segregated schools through any arrangement . . . cannot be squared with the Amendment's command that no State shall deny to any person within its jurisdiction the equal protection of the laws.   The Justices of the Court (1958)

Court-Ordered Busing

Swann v. Board of Education
95

In these circumstances, we find no basis for holding that the local school authorities may not be required to employ bus transportation as one tool of school desegregation. Desegregation plans cannot be limited to the walk-in school.

Chief Justice Warren Burger (1971)

THE RIGHT TO VOTE

The Texas Election Cases
Nixon I
123

What is this but declaring that the law in the States shall be the same for the black as for the white; that all persons, whether colored or white, shall stand equal before the laws of the States, and, in regard to the colored race, for whose protection the [Fourteenth] amendment was primarily designed, that no discrimination shall be made against them by law because of their color?

Justice Oliver Wendell Holmes, Jr. (1927)

Nixon II
128

The Fourteenth Amendment, adopted as it was with special solicitude for the equal protection of members of the Negro race, lays a duty upon the court to level by its judgment these barriers of color.

Justice Benjamin Cardozo (1932)

PUBLIC TRANSPORTATION

The Woman Who Would Not Go To The Back of the Bus

Irene Morgan v. Virginia
139

No state can reach beyond its own border nor bar transportation of passengers across its boundaries. . . . It seems clear to us that seating arrangements for the different races in interstate motor travel require a single, uniform rule to promote and protect national travel.

Justice Stanley Reed (1946)

RACIALLY RESTRICTED HOUSING

Shelly v. Kraemer
149

The Constitution confers upon no individual the right to demand action by the State which results in the denial of equal protection of the laws to other individuals.

Chief Justice Fredrick Vinson (1948)

PUBLIC ACCOMMODATIONS

Heart Of Atlanta Motel v. United States
167

That Congress was legislating against moral wrongs in many of these areas rendered its enactments no less valid. In framing Title II (of the Civil Rights Act of 1964) Congress was also dealing with what it considered a moral problem. But that does not detract from the overwhelming evidence of the disruptive effect that racial discrimination has had on commercial intercourse.

Justice Tom Clark (1964)

INTERRACIAL MARRIAGE

Loving v. Virginia
187

Marriage is one of the "basic civil rights of man," fundamental to our very existence. . . . The Fourteenth Amendment requires that the freedom of choice to marry not be restricted by invidious racial discriminations. Under our Constitution, the freedom to marry, or not marry, a person of another race resides with the individual and cannot be infringed by the State.

Chief Justice Earl Warren (1967)

AFFIRMATIVE ACTION

Regents of the University of California v. Allan Bakke
199

The guarantee of equal protection cannot mean one thing when applied to one individual and something else when applied to a person of another color. If both are not accorded the same protection, then it is not equal.

Justice Lewis Powell (1978)

U.S. Constitution
231

THE JAPANESE AMERICAN INTERNMENT CASES

Hirabayashi v. United States

[T]he successful prosecution of the war requires every possible protection against espionage and sabotage to national defense. . . . [By virtue of the authority vested in me as President of the United States and as Commander in Chief of the Army and Navy I, Franklin D. Roosevelt] authorize and direct the Secretary of War . . . whenever he deems such action necessary or desirable, to prescribe military areas in such places . . . from which any and all persons may be excluded.

Executive Order 9066

On February 19, 1942, six weeks after Japan's attack on Pearl Harbor, President Franklin Roosevelt issued Executive Order 9066 authorizing the U.S. Army to exclude Japanese Americans from designated areas along the Pacific Coast. On March 21, 1942 the U.S. Congress passed the Exclusion Act, making resistance to Executive Order 9066 a crime. On March 24, 1942 General John DeWitt, Western Defense Military Commander, issued Public Proclamations Nos. 1 and 2, designating Military Exclusion Zones. Public Proclamation No. 3 directed all persons of Japanese ancestry within the Military Exclusion Area, preliminary to their relocation, to obey a curfew in effect between the hours of 8:00 p.m. and 6 a.m. On May 9, 1942 Gordon Hirabayashi, a Japanese American living in Seattle, Washington, violated the curfew order. He was tried in Federal Court, found guilty, and sentenced to three months in prison. Hirabayashi, asserting that the Exclusion Act was unconstitutional under the Fifth Amendment, appealed to the United States Court of Appeals, which referred the case to the U.S. Supreme Court.

On June 21, 1943 Chief Justice Harlan Fiske Stone announced the Court's 9-0 decision. The edited text follows.

THE HIRABAYASHI COURT

Chief Justice Harlan Fiske Stone
Appointed by President Coolidge
Served 1925 - 1946

Associate Justice Owen Roberts
Appointed by President Hoover
Served 1930 - 1945

Associate Justice Hugo Black
Appointed by President Franklin Roosevelt
Served 1937 - 1971

Associate Justice Stanley Reed
Appointed by President Franklin Roosevelt
Served 1938 - 1957

Associate Justice Felix Frankfurter
Appointed by President Franklin Roosevelt
Served 1939 - 1962

Associate Justice William O. Douglas
Appointed by President Franklin Roosevelt
Served 1939 - 1975

Associate Justice Frank Murphy
Appointed by President Franklin Roosevelt
Served 1940 - 1949

Associate Justice Robert Jackson
Appointed by President Franklin Roosevelt
Served 1941 - 1954

Associate Justice Wiley Rutledge
Appointed by President Franklin Roosevelt
Served 1943 - 1949

The unedited text of *Hirabayashi v. United States* can be found on page 81, volume 320 of *United States Reports*.

HIRABAYASHI v. UNITED STATES
June 21, 1943

CHIEF JUSTICE STONE: Appellant [Gordon Hirabayashi], an American citizen of Japanese ancestry, was convicted . . . of violating the Act of Congress of March 21, 1942, which makes it a misdemeanor knowingly to disregard restrictions made applicable by a military commander to persons in a military area prescribed by him as such, all as authorized by an Executive Order of the President.

The questions for our decision are whether the particular restriction violated, namely that all persons of Japanese ancestry residing in such an area be within their place of residence daily between the hours of 8:00 p.m. and 6:00 a.m., was adopted by the military commander in the exercise of an unconstitutional delegation by Congress of its legislative power, and whether the restriction unconstitutionally discriminated between citizens of Japanese ancestry and those of other ancestries in violation of the Fifth Amendment.

The indictment . . . charges that [Hirabayashi], being a person of Japanese ancestry, had on a specified date, contrary to a restriction promulgated by the military commander of the Western Defense Command, Fourth Army, failed to remain in his place of residence in the designated military area between the hours of 8:00 o'clock p.m. and 6:00 a.m. The first count charges that [Hirabayashi], on May 11 and 12, 1942, had, contrary to a Civilian Exclusion Order issued by the military commander, failed to report to the Civil Control Station within the designated area, it appearing that [Hirabayashi]'s required presence there was a preliminary step to the exclusion from that area of persons of Japanese ancestry.

. . . . [Hirabayashi] asserted that the indictment should be dismissed because he was an American citizen who had never been a subject of and had never borne allegiance to the Empire of Japan, and also because the Act of March 21, 1942, was an unconstitutional delegation of Congressional power. On the trial to a jury it appeared that [Hirabayashi] was born in Seattle in 1918, of Japanese parents who had come from Japan to the United States, and who had never afterward returned to Japan; that he was educated in the Washington public schools and at the time of his arrest was a senior in the University of Washington; that he had never been in Japan or had any association with Japanese residing there.

The evidence showed that [Hirabayashi] had failed to report to the Civil Control Station on May 11 or May 12, 1942, as directed, to register for evacuation from the military area. He admitted failure to do so, and stated it had at all times been his belief that he would be waiving his rights as an American citizen by so doing. The evidence also showed that for like reason he was away from his place of residence after 8:00 p.m. on May 9, 1942. The jury returned a verdict of guilty on both counts and [Hirabayashi] was sentenced to imprisonment for a term of three months on each, the sentences to run concurrently.

On appeal the [United States] Court of Appeals [asked us for] instructions for the decision of the case.

The curfew order which [Hirabayashi] violated, and to which the sanction prescribed by the Act of Congress has been deemed to attach, purported to be issued pursuant to an Executive Order of the President. In passing upon the authority of the military commander to make and execute the order, it becomes necessary to consider in some detail the official action which preceded or accompanied the order and from which it derives its purported authority.

On December 8, 1941, one day after the bombing of Pearl Harbor by a Japanese air force, Congress declared war against Japan. On February 19, 1942, the President promulgated Executive Order No. 9066. The Order recited that "the successful prosecution of the war requires every possible protection against espionage and against sabotage to national-defense material, national-defense premises, and national-defense utilities. . . ." By virtue of the authority vested in him as President and as Commander in Chief of the Army and Navy, the President purported to

> "authorize and direct the Secretary of War, and the Military Commanders whom he may from time to time designate, whenever he or any designated Commander deems such action necessary or desirable, to prescribe military areas in such places and of such extent as he or the appropriate Military Commander may determine, from which any or all persons may be excluded, and with respect to which, the right of any person to enter, remain in, or leave shall be subject to whatever restrictions the Secretary of War or the appropriate Military Commander may impose in his discretion."

On February 20, 1942, the Secretary of War designated Lt. General J.L. DeWitt as Military Commander of the Western Defense Command, comprising the Pacific Coast states and some others, to carry out there the duties prescribed by Executive Order No. 9066. On March 2, 1942, General DeWitt promulgated Public Proclamation No. 1. The proclamation recited that the entire Pacific Coast "by its geographical location is particularly subject to attack, to attempted invasion by the armed forces of nations with which the United States is now at war, and, in connection therewith, is subject to espionage and acts of sabotage, thereby requiring the adoption of military measures necessary to establish safeguards against such enemy operations." It stated that "the present situation requires as a matter of military necessity the establishment in the territory embraced by the Western Defense Command of Military Areas and Zones thereof"; it specified and designated as military areas certain areas within the Western Defense Command; and it declared that "such persons or classes of persons as the situation may require" would, by subsequent proclamation, be excluded from certain of these areas, but might be permitted to enter or remain in certain others, under regulations and restrictions to be later prescribed. Among the military areas so designated by Public Proclamation No. 1 was Military Area No. 1, which embraced, besides the southern part of Arizona, all the coastal region of the three Pacific Coast states, including the City of Seattle, Washington, where [Hirabayashi] resided.
. . .

Public Proclamation No. 2 of March 16, 1942, issued by General DeWitt, made like recitals and designated further military areas and zones. It contained like provisions concerning the exclusion, by subsequent proclamation, of certain persons or classes of persons from these areas, and the future promulgation of regulations and restrictions applicable to persons remaining within them.

. . . . Congress, by the Act of March 21, 1942, provided: "That whoever shall enter, remain in, leave, or commit any act in any military area or military zone prescribed, under the authority of an Executive order of the President, by the Secretary of War, or by any military commander designated by the Secretary of War, contrary to the restrictions applicable to any such area or zone or contrary to the order of the Secretary of War or any such military commander, shall, if it appears that he knew or should have known of the existence and extent of the restrictions or order and that his act was in violation thereof, be guilty of a misdemeanor and upon conviction shall be liable" to fine or imprisonment, or both.

Three days later, On March 24, 1942, General DeWitt issued Public Proclamation No. 3. After referring to the previous designation of military areas by Public Proclamations Nos. 1 and 2, it recited that ". . . the present situation within these Military Areas and Zones requires as a matter of military necessity the establishment of certain regulations pertaining to all enemy aliens and all persons of Japanese ancestry within said Military Areas and Zones. . . ." It accordingly declared and established that from and after March 27, 1942, "all alien Japanese, all alien Germans, all alien Italians, and all persons of Japanese ancestry residing or being within the geographical limits of Military Area No. 1 . . . shall be within their place of residence between the hours of 8:00 P.M. and 6:00 A.M., which period is hereinafter referred to as the hours of curfew." It also imposed certain other restrictions on persons of Japanese ancestry, and provided that any person violating the regulations would be subject to the criminal penalties provided by the Act of Congress of March 21, 1942.

Beginning on March 24, 1942, the military commander issued a series of Civilian Exclusion Orders pursuant to the provisions of Public Proclamation No. 1. Each such order related to a specified area within the territory of his command. The order applicable to [Hirabayashi] was Civilian Exclusion Order No. 57 of May 10, 1942. It directed that from and after 12:00 noon, May 16, 1942, all persons of Japanese ancestry, both alien and non-alien, be excluded from a specified portion of Military Area No. 1 in Seattle, including [Hirabayashi]'s place of residence, and it required a member of each family, and each individual living alone, affected by the order to report on May 11 or May 12 to a designated Civil Control Station in Seattle. Meanwhile the military commander had issued Public Proclamation No. 4 of March 27, 1942, which recited the necessity of providing for the orderly evacuation and resettlement of Japanese within the area, and prohibited all alien Japanese and all persons of Japanese ancestry from leaving the military area until future orders should permit.

[Hirabayashi] does not deny that he knowingly failed to obey the curfew order as charged . . . , or that the order was authorized by the terms of Executive Order No. 9066, or that the challenged Act of Congress purports to punish with criminal penalties disobedience of such an order. His contentions are only that Congress unconstitutionally delegated its legislative power to the military commander by authorizing him to impose the challenged regulation, and that, even if the regulation were in other respects lawfully authorized, the Fifth Amendment prohibits the discrimination made between citizens of Japanese descent and those of other ancestry.

. . . . [Hirabayashi] does not deny that, given the danger, a curfew was an appropriate measure against sabotage. It is an obvious protection against the perpetration of sabotage most readily committed during the hours of darkness. If it was an appropriate exercise of the war power its validity is not impaired because it has restricted the citizen's liberty. Like every military control of the population of a dangerous zone in war time, it necessarily involves some infringement of individual liberty, just as does the police establishment of fire lines during a fire, or the confinement of people to their houses during an air raid alarm - neither of which could be thought to be an infringement of constitutional right. Like them, the validity of the restraints of the curfew order depends on all the conditions which obtain at the time the curfew is imposed and which support the order imposing it.

But [Hirabayashi] insists that the exercise of the power is inappropriate and unconstitutional because it discriminates against citizens of Japanese ancestry, in violation of the Fifth Amendment. The Fifth Amendment contains no equal protection clause and it restrains only such discriminatory legislation by Congress as amounts to a denial of due process. . . .

Distinctions between citizens solely because of their ancestry are by their very nature odious to a free people whose institutions are founded upon the doctrine of equality. For that reason, legislative classification or discrimination based on race alone has often been held to be a denial of equal protection. We may assume that these considerations would be controlling here were it not for the fact that the danger of espionage and sabotage, in time of war and of threatened invasion, calls upon the military authorities to scrutinize every relevant fact bearing on the loyalty of populations in the danger areas. Because racial discriminations are in most circumstances irrelevant and therefore prohibited, it by no means follows that, in dealing with the perils of war, Congress and the Executive are wholly precluded from taking into account those facts and circumstances which are relevant to measures for our national defense and for the successful prosecution of the war, and which may in fact place citizens of one ancestry in a different category from others. "We must never forget, that it is *a constitution* we are expounding," "a constitution intended to endure for ages to come, and, consequently, to be adapted to the various *crises* of human affairs." The adoption by Government, in the crisis of war and of threatened invasion, of measures for the public safety, based upon the recognition of facts and circumstances which indicate that a group of one national extraction may menace that safety more than others, is not wholly beyond the limits of the Constitution and is not to be condemned merely because in other and in most circumstances racial distinctions are irrelevant.

Here the aim of Congress and the Executive was the protection against sabotage of war materials and utilities in areas thought to be in danger of Japanese invasion and air attack. We have stated in detail facts and circumstances with respect to the American citizens of Japanese ancestry residing on the Pacific Coast which support the judgment of the war-waging branches of the Government that some restrictive measure was urgent. We cannot say that these facts and circumstances, considered in the particular war setting, could afford no ground for differentiating citizens of Japanese ancestry from other groups in the United States. The fact alone that attack on our shores was threatened by Japan rather than another enemy power set these citizens apart from others who have no particular associations with Japan.

Our investigation here does not go beyond the inquiry whether, in the light of all the relevant circumstances preceding and attending their promulgation, the challenged orders and statute afforded a reasonable basis for the action taken in imposing the curfew. We cannot close our eyes to the fact, demonstrated by experience, that in time of war residents having ethnic affiliations with an invading enemy may be a greater source of danger than those of a different ancestry. Nor can we deny that Congress, and the military authorities acting with its authorization, have constitutional power to appraise the danger in the light of facts of public notoriety. We need not now attempt to define the ultimate boundaries of the war power. We decide only the issue as we have defined it - we decide only that the curfew order as applied, and at the time it was applied, was within the boundaries of the war power. In this case it is enough that circumstances within the knowledge of those charged with the responsibility for maintaining the national defense afforded a rational basis for the decision which they made. Whether we would have made it is irrelevant.

What we have said also disposes of the contention that the curfew order involved an unlawful delegation by Congress of its legislative power. The mandate of the Constitution that all legislative power granted "shall be vested in Congress" has never been thought, even in the administration of civil affairs, to preclude Congress from resorting to the aid of executive or administrative officers in determining by findings whether the facts are such as to call for the application of previously adopted legislative standards or definitions of Congressional policy.

The purpose of Executive Order No. 9066, and the standard which the President approved for the orders authorized to be promulgated by the military commander - as disclosed by the preamble of the Executive Order - was the protection of our war resources against espionage and sabotage. Public Proclamations Nos. 1 and 2 by General DeWitt, contain findings that the military areas created and the measures to be prescribed for them were required to establish safeguards against espionage and sabotage. Both the Executive Order and the Proclamations were before Congress when the Act of March 21, 1942, was under consideration. To the extent that the Executive Order authorized orders to be promulgated by the military commander to accomplish the declared purpose of the Order, and to the extent that the findings in the Proclamations establish that such was their purpose, both have been approved by Congress.

.... The military commander's appraisal of facts in the light of the authorized standard, and the inferences which he drew from those facts, involved the exercise of his informed judgment. But as we have seen, those facts, and the inferences which could be rationally drawn from them, support the judgment of the military commander, that the danger of espionage and sabotage to our military resources was imminent, and that the curfew order was an appropriate measure to meet it.

Where, as in the present case, the standard set up for the guidance of the military commander, and the action taken and the reasons for it, are in fact recorded in the military orders, so that Congress, the courts and the public are assured that the orders, in the judgment of the commander, conform to the standards approved by the President and Congress, there is no failure in the performance of the legislative function. The essentials of that function are the determination by Congress of the legislative policy and its approval of a rule of conduct to carry that policy into execution. The very necessities which attend the conduct of military operations in time of war in this instance as in many others preclude Congress from holding committee meetings to determine whether there is danger, before it enacts legislation to combat the danger.

The Constitution as a continuously operating charter of government does not demand the impossible or the impractical. The essentials of the legislative function are preserved when Congress authorizes a statutory command to become operative, upon ascertainment of a basic conclusion of fact by a designated representative of the Government. The present statute, which authorized curfew orders to be made pursuant to Executive Order No. 9066 for the protection of war resources from espionage and sabotage, satisfies those requirements. Under the Executive Order the basic facts, determined by the military commander in the light of knowledge then available, were whether that danger existed and whether a curfew order was an appropriate means of minimizing the danger. Since his findings to that effect were, as we have said, not without adequate support, the legislative function was performed and the sanction of the statute attached to violations of the curfew order. It is unnecessary to consider whether or to what extent such findings would support orders differing from the curfew order.

The conviction . . . is without constitutional infirmity. . . . Affirmed [upheld].

THE JAPANESE AMERICAN INTERNMENT CASES

Korematsu v. United States

[W]hoever shall enter, remain in, leave, or commit any act in any military area or military zone prescribed, under the authority of an Executive order of the President, by the Secretary of War, or by any military commander designated by the Secretary of War, contrary to the restrictions applicable to any such area or zone or contrary to the order of the secretary of War or any such military commander, shall, if it appears that he knew or should have known of the existence and extent of the restrictions or order and that his act was in violation thereof, be guilty of a misdemeanor and upon conviction shall be liable to a fine of not to exceed $5,000 or to imprisonment for not more than a year, or both, for each offense.

The Japanese American Exclusion Act

In response to President Roosevelt's February 19, 1942 Executive Order No. 9066, the U.S. Congress passed, on March 21, 1942, the Japanese American Exclusion Act. The Exclusion Act authorized the Secretary of War to exclude any and all persons from certain military areas in order to protect military installations from espionage and sabotage. On May 9, 1942 Civilian Exclusion Order No. 34, signed by General John DeWitt, Commanding General, Western Defense Command, directed all persons of Japanese ancestry, without reference to their loyalty, to be excluded from San Leandro, California. Fred Toyosaburo Korematsu, an American citizen of Japanese ancestry living in San Leandro, refused to leave. Korematsu was tried and convicted in a Federal District Court of violating the Exclusion Act. An Appeals Court upheld his conviction. Korematsu appealed to the U.S. Supreme Court.

On December 18, 1944 Justice Hugo Black announced the 6-3 decision of the Court. The edited text follows.

THE KOREMATSU COURT

Chief Justice Harlan Fiske Stone
Appointed by President Coolidge
Served 1925 - 1946

Associate Justice Owen Roberts
Appointed by President Hoover
Served 1930 - 1945

Associate Justice Hugo Black
Appointed by President Franklin Roosevelt
Served 1937 - 1971

Associate Justice Stanley Reed
Appointed by President Franklin Roosevelt
Served 1938 - 1957

Associate Justice Felix Frankfurter
Appointed by President Franklin Roosevelt
Served 1939 - 1962

Associate Justice William O. Douglas
Appointed by President Franklin Roosevelt
Served 1939 - 1975

Associate Justice Frank Murphy
Appointed by President Franklin Roosevelt
Served 1940 - 1949

Associate Justice Robert Jackson
Appointed by President Franklin Roosevelt
Served 1941 - 1954

Associate Justice Wiley Rutledge
Appointed by President Franklin Roosevelt
Served 1943 - 1949

The unedited text of *Korematsu v. United States* can be found on page 214, volume 323 of *United States Reports*.

KOREMATSU v. UNITED STATES
December 18, 1944

JUSTICE HUGO BLACK: The petitioner [Fred Toyosaburo Korematsu], an American citizen of Japanese descent, was convicted in a federal district court for remaining in San Leandro, California, a "Military Area," contrary to Civilian Exclusion Order No. 34 of the Commanding General of the Western Command, U.S. Army, which directed that after May 9, 1942, all persons of Japanese ancestry should be excluded from that area. No question was raised as to [Korematsu]'s loyalty to the United States....

It should be noted, to begin with, that all legal restrictions which curtail the civil rights of a single racial group are immediately suspect. That is not to say that all such restrictions are unconstitutional. It is to say that courts must subject them to the most rigid scrutiny. Pressing public necessity may sometimes justify the existence of such restrictions; racial antagonism never can.

In [this] case prosecution of [Korematsu] was begun by [the obtaining of] information charging violation of an Act of Congress, of March 21, 1942, which provides that "... whoever shall enter, remain in, leave, or commit any act in any military area or military zone prescribed, under the authority of an Executive order of the President, by the Secretary of War, or by any military commander designated by the Secretary of War, contrary to the restrictions applicable to any such area or zone or contrary to the order of the Secretary of War or any such military commander, shall, if it appears that he knew or should have known of the existence and extent of the restrictions or order and that his act was in violation thereof, be guilty of a misdemeanor and upon conviction shall be li-

able to a fine of not to exceed $5,000 or to imprisonment
for not more than one year, or both, for each offense."

Exclusion Order No. 34, which [Korematsu] knowingly
and admittedly violated, was one of a number of military
orders and proclamations, all of which were substantially
based upon Executive Order No. 9066. That order, issued
after we were at war with Japan, declared that "the successful prosecution of the war requires every possible protection against espionage and against sabotage to national-
defense material, national-defense premises, and national-
defense utilities. . . ."

One of the series of orders and proclamations, a curfew
order . . . subjected all persons of Japanese ancestry in
prescribed West Coast military areas to remain in their
residences from 8 p.m. to 6 a.m. . . . [T]hat . . . curfew order was designed as a "protection against espionage and
against sabotage." In *Hirabayashi v. United States,* we sustained [maintained] a conviction obtained for violation of
the curfew order. The *Hirabayashi* conviction and this
one thus rest on the same 1942 Congressional Act and the
same basic executive and military orders, all of which orders were aimed at the twin dangers of espionage and
sabotage.

The 1942 Act was attacked in the *Hirabayashi* Case as an
unconstitutional delegation of power; it was contended
that the curfew order and other orders on which it rested
were beyond the war powers of the Congress, the military
authorities and of the President, as Commander in Chief
of the Army; and finally that to apply the curfew order
against none but citizens of Japanese ancestry amounted
to a constitutionally prohibited discrimination solely on
account of race. To these questions, we gave the serious

consideration which their importance justified. We upheld the curfew order as an exercise of the power of the
government to take steps necessary to prevent espionage
and sabotage in an area threatened by Japanese attack.

In the light of the principles we announced in the *Hirabayashi* Case, we are unable to conclude that it was beyond the war power of Congress and the Executive to exclude those of Japanese ancestry from the West Coast war
area at the time they did. True, exclusion from the area
in which one's home is located is a far greater deprivation
than constant confinement to the home from 8 p.m. to 6
a.m. Nothing short of apprehension by the proper military authorities of the gravest imminent danger to the
public safety can constitutionally justify either. But exclusion from a threatened area, no less than curfew, has a
definite and close relationship to the prevention of espionage and sabotage. The military authorities, charged with
the primary responsibility of defending our shores, concluded that curfew provided inadequate protection and ordered exclusion. They did so, as pointed out in our *Hirabayashi* opinion, in accordance with congressional authority to the military to say who should, and who should not,
remain in the threatened areas.

In this case [Korematsu] challenges the assumptions upon
which we rested our conclusions in the *Hirabayashi* Case.
He also urges that by May 1942, when Order No. 34 was
promulgated, all danger of Japanese invastion of the West
Coast had disappeared. After careful consideration of
these contentions we are compelled to reject them.

Here, as in the *Hirabayashi* Case, "we cannot reject as un-
founded the judgment of the military authorities and of
Congress that there were disloyal members of that popula-

tion, whose number and strength could not be precisely and quickly ascertained. We cannot say that the war-making branches of the Government did not have ground for believing that in a critical hour such persons could not readily be isolated and separately dealt with, and constituted a menace to the national defense and safety, which demanded that prompt and adequate measures be taken to guard against it."

Like curfew, exclusion of those of Japanese origin was deemed necessary because of the presence of an unascertained number of disloyal members of the group, most of whom we have no doubt were loyal to this country. It was because we could not reject the finding of the military authorities that it was impossible to bring about an immediate segregation of the disloyal from the loyal that we sustained the validity of the curfew order as applying to the whole group. In [this] case, temporary exclusion of the entire group was rested by the military on the same ground. The judgment that exclusion of the whole group was for the same reason a military imperative answers the contention that the exclusion was in the nature of group punishment based on antagonism to those of Japanese origin. That there were members of the group who retained loyalties to Japan has been confirmed by investigations made subsequent to the exclusion. Approximately five thousand American citizens of Japanese ancestry refused to swear unqualified allegiance to the United States and to renounce allegiance to the Japanese Emperor, and several thousand evacuees requested repatriation to Japan.

We uphold the exclusion order as of the time it was made and when [Korematsu] violated it. In doing so, we are not unmindful of the hardships imposed by it upon a large group of American citizens. But hardships are part of war, and war is an aggregation of hardships. All citizens alike, both in and out of uniform, feel the impact of war in greater or lesser measure. Citizenship has its responsibilities as well as its privileges, and in time of war the burden is always heavier. Compulsory exclusion of large groups of citizens from their homes, except under circumstances of direst emergency and peril, is inconsistent with our basic governmental institutions. But when under conditions of modern warfare our shores are threatened by hostile forces, the power to protect must be commensurate with the threatened danger.

It is argued that on May 30, 1942, the date [Korematsu] was charged with remaining in the prohibited area, there were conflicting orders outstanding, forbidding him both to leave the area and to remain there. Of course, a person cannot be convicted for doing the very thing which it is a crime to fail to do. But the outstanding orders here contained no such contradictory commands.

There was an order issued March 27, 1942, which prohibited [Korematsu] and others of Japanese ancestry from leaving the area, but its effect was specifically limited in time "until and to the extent that a future proclamation or order should so permit or direct." That "future order," the one for violation of which [Korematsu] was convicted, was issued May 3, 1942, and it did "direct" exclusion from the area of all persons of Japanese ancestry, before 12 o'clock noon, May 9; furthermore it contained a warning that all such persons found in the prohibited area would be liable to punishment under the March 21, 1942 Act of Congress. Consequently, the only order in effect touching [Korematsu]'s being in the area on May 30, 1942, the date specified in the information against him, was the May 3 order which prohibited his remaining there, and it was that same order, which he stipulated in his trial that he had violated, knowing of its existence. There is therefore no basis for the argument that on May 30, 1942, he was subject to punishment, under the March 27 and May 3 orders, whether he remained in or left the area.

It does appear, however, that on May 9, the effective date of the exclusion order, the military authorities had already determined that the evacuation should be effected by assembling together and placing under guard all those of Japanese ancestry, at central points, designated as "assembly centers," in order "to insure the orderly evacuation and resettlement of Japanese voluntarily migrating from military area No. 1 to restrict and regulate such migration." And on May 19, 1942, eleven days before the time petitioner was charged with unlawfully remaining in the area, Civilian Restrictive Order No. 1 provided for detention of those of Japanese ancestry in assembly or relocation centers. It is now argued that the validity of the exclusion order cannot be considered apart from the orders requiring him, after departure from the area, to report and to remain in an assembly or relocation center. The contention is that we must treat these separate orders as one and inseparable; that, for this reason, if detention in the assembly or relocation center would have illegally deprived [Korematsu] of his liberty, the exclusion order and his conviction under it cannot stand.

We are thus being asked to pass at this time upon the whole subsequent detention program in both assembly and relocation centers, although the only issues framed at the trial related to [Korematsu]'s remaining in the prohibited area in violation of the exclusion order. Had [Korematsu] left the prohibited area and gone to an assembly center we cannot say either as a matter of fact or law, that his

presence in that center would have resulted in his detention in a relocation center. . . .

Since [Korematsu] has not been convicted of failing to report or to remain in an assembly or relocation center, we
cannot in this case determine the validity of those separate provisions of the order. It is sufficient here for us to
pass upon the order which [Korematsu] violated. . . . It
will be time enough to decide the serious constitutional
issues which [he] seeks to raise when an assembly or relocation order is applied or is certain to be applied to him,
and we have its terms before us.

Some of the members of the Court are of the view that
evacuation and detention in an Assembly Center were inseparable. After May 3, 1942, the date of Exclusion Order No. 34, Korematsu was under compulsion to leave the
area not as he would choose but via an Assembly Center.
The Assembly Center was conceived as a part of the machinery for group evacuation. The power to exclude includes the power to do it by force if necessary. And any
forcible measure must necessarily entail some degree of
detention or restraint whatever method of removal is selected. But whichever view is taken, it results in holding
that the order under which [Korematsu] was convicted
was valid.

It is said that we are dealing here with the case of imprisonment of a citizen in a concentration camp solely because of his ancestry, without evidence or inquiry concerning his loyalty and good disposition towards the United States. Our task would be simple, our duty clear, were
this a case involving the imprisonment of a loyal citizen
in a concentration camp because of racial prejudice. Regardless of the true nature of the assembly and relocation

centers - and we deem it unjustifiable to call them concentration camps with all the ugly connotations that term implies - we are dealing specifically with nothing but an exclusion order. To cast this case into outlines of racial prejudice, without reference to the real military dangers which were presented, merely confuses the issue. Korematsu was not excluded from the Military Area because of hostility to him or his race. He *was* excluded because we are at war with the Japanese Empire, because the properly constituted military authorities feared an invasion of our West Coast and felt constrained to take proper security measures, because they decided that the military urgency of the situation demanded that all citizens of Japanese ancestry be segregated from the West Coast temporarily, and finally, because Congress, reposing its confidence in this time of war in our military leaders - as inevitably it must - determined that they should have the power to do just this. There was evidence of disloyalty on the part of some, the military authorities considered that the need for action was great, and time was short. We cannot - by availing ourselves of the calm perspective of hindsight - now say that at that time these actions were unjustified. Affirmed [upheld].

In 1983 the American Civil Liberties Union and the Japanese American Citizens League presented to a United States District Court testimony that the United States government had suppressed evidence in the Korematsu *case. U.S. District Court Judge Marilyn Hall Patel vacated the Korematsu conviction.*

MOB JUSTICE

Moore v. Dempsey

[A] deliberately planned insurrection [in Elaine, Arkansas] . . . for the purpose of banding negroes together for the killing of white people. **The Committee of Seven**

On the night of September 30, 1919 in a church near Elaine, Arkansas, a group of black sharecroppers holding a meeting were attacked by a white mob. In the fight that followed, one white man was killed. Five black men, Frank Moore, Ed Hicks, J.E. Knox, Ed Coleman, and Paul Hall, were arrested for murder. Lynch mobs gathered. Federal troops were called out. A "Committee of Seven," appointed by the Governor to investigate the "Elaine Insurrection," made a "solemn promise" to the public that "they would execute those found guilty." On November 3 the Elaine Five went on trial at the Phillips County Courthouse, which was surrounded on all sides by an angry mob. The trial, before an all-white jury, lasted forty-five minutes. The prosecution offered the testimony of two witnesses tortured into testifying by the Committee. The Court-appointed defense lawyer, who had never spoken to the defendants, had not requested a delay, or a change of venue, nor challenged the selection of the jury. He called no witnesses and did not put the defendants on the stand. The jury deliberated less than five minutes. The Five were found guilty of murder and sentenced to die. Exhausting their appeals in the Arkansas Courts, they appealed to a Federal Court. On the basis of being denied due process, they asked for and were denied a writ of *habeas corpus* forcing Warden Dempsey of the Arkansas State Penitentiary to surrender them into federal custody. The Five appealed to the U.S. Supreme Court.

On February 19, 1923 Associate Justice Oliver Wendell Holmes, Jr. announced the 7-2 decision of the Court. The edited text follows.

THE MOORE COURT

Chief Justice William Howard Taft
Appointed by President Harding
Served 1921 - 1930

Associate Justice Joseph McKenna
Appointed by President McKinley
Served 1898 - 1925

Associate Justice Oliver Wendell Holmes, Jr.
Appointed by President Theodore Roosevelt
Served 1902 - 1932

Associate Justice Willis Van Devanter
Appointed by President Taft
Served 1910 - 1937

Associate Justice James McReynolds
Appointed by President Wilson
Served 1914 - 1941

Associate Justice Louis Brandeis
Appointed by President Wilson
Served 1916 - 1939

Associate Justice George Sutherland
Appointed by President Harding
Served 1922 - 1938

Associate Justice Pierce Butler
Appointed by President Harding
Served 1922 - 1939

Associate Justice Edward Sanford
Appointed by President Harding
Served 1923 - 1930

The unedited text of *Moore v. Dempsey* can be found on page 86, volume 261 of *United States Reports*.

MOORE v. DEMPSEY
February 19, 1923

JUSTICE HOLMES: .... On the night of September 30, 1919, a number of colored people assembled in their church were attacked and fired upon by a body of white men, and in the disturbance that followed a white man was killed. The report of the killing caused great excitement and was followed by the hunting down and shooting of many negroes and also by the killing on October 1 of one Clinton Lee, a white man, for whose murder the petitioners [Moore and others] were indicted [charged]. They seem to have been arrested with many others on the same day. [Moore says] that Lee must have been killed by other whites, but that we leave on one side as what we have to deal with is not [Moore's] innocence or guilt but solely the question whether [his] constitutional rights have been preserved. [Moore says] that their meeting was to employ counsel for protection against extortions practiced upon them by the landowners and that the landowners tried to prevent their effort, but that again we pass by as not directly bearing upon the trial. It should be mentioned however that O.S. Bratton, a son of the counsel who is said to have been contemplated and who took part in the argument here, arriving for consultation on October 1, is said to have barely escaped being mobbed; that he was arrested and confined during the month on a charge of murder and on October 31 was indicted for barratry [starting a fight], but later in the day was told that he would be discharged but that he must leave secretly by a closed automobile to take the train at West Helena, four miles away, to avoid being mobbed. It is alleged that the judge of the Court in which the petitioners were tried facilitated the departure and went with Bratton to see him safely off.

A Committee of Seven was appointed by the Governor in regard to what the committee called the "insurrection" in the county. The newspapers daily published inflammatory articles. On the 7th a statement by one of the committee was made public to the effect that the present was "a deliberately planned insurrection of the negroes against the whites, directed by an organization known as the 'Progressive Farmers' and Household Union of America' established for the purpose of banding negroes together for the killing of white people." According to the statement the organization was started by a swindler to get money from the blacks.

Shortly after the arrest of [Moore and the others] a mob marched to the jail for the purpose of lynching them but were prevented by the presence of United States troops and the promise of some of the Committee of Seven and other leading officials that if the mob would refrain, as the petition puts it, they would execute those found guilty in the form of law. The Committee's own statement was that the reason that the people refrained from mob violence was "that this Committee gave our citizens their solemn promise that the law would be carried out." According to affidavits [sworn statements] of two white men and the colored witnesses on whose testimony the petitioners were convicted, produced by the petitioners since the last decision of the Supreme Court hereafter mentioned, the Committee made good their promise by calling colored witnesses and having them whipped and tortured until they would say what was wanted, among them being the two relied on to prove the petitioners' guilt. However this may be, a grand jury of white men was organized on October 27 with one of the Committee of Seven and, it is alleged, with many of a posse organized to fight the blacks, upon it, and on the morning of the 29th the indictment was returned. On November 3 the petitioners were brought into Court, informed that a certain lawyer was appointed their counsel and were placed on trial before a white jury - blacks being systematically excluded from both grand and petit juries. The Court and neighborhood were thronged with an adverse crowd that threatened the most dangerous consequences to anyone interfering with the desired result. The counsel did not venture to demand delay or a change of venue [place where a case is heard], to challenge a juryman or to ask for separate trials. He had had no preliminary consultation with the accused, called no witnesses for the defence although they could have been produced, and did not put the defendants on the stand. The trial lasted about three-quarters of an hour and in less than five minutes the jury brought in a verdict of guilty of murder in the first degree. According to the allegations and affidavits there never was a chance for the petitioners to be acquitted [found innocent]; no juryman could have voted for an acquittal and continued to live in Phillips County and if any prisoner by any chance had been acquitted by a jury he could not have escaped the mob.

The averments [statements] as to the prejudice by which the trial was environed have some corroboration in appeals to the Governor, about a year later, earnestly urging him not to interfere with the execution of the petitioners. One came from five members of the Committee of Seven, and stated in addition to what has been quoted heretofore that "all our citizens are of the opinion that the law should take its course." Another from a part of the American Legion protests against a contemplated commutation of the sentence of four of the petitioners and repeats that a "solemn promise was given by the leading citizens of the community that if the guilty parties were not lynched, and let the law take its course, that justice would be done and the majesty of the law upheld." A meeting of the Helena Rotary Club attended by members representing, as it said, seventy-five of the leading industrial and commercial enterprises of Helena, passed a resolution approving and supporting the action of the American Legion post. The Lions Club of Helena at a meeting attended by members said to represent sixty of the leading industrial and commercial enterprises of the city passed a resolution to the same effect. In May of the same year, a trial of six other negroes was coming on and it was represented to the Governor by the white citizens and officials of Phillips County that in all probability those negroes would be lynched. It is alleged that in order to appease the mob spirit and in a measure secure the safety of the six the Governor fixed the date for the execution of the petitioners at June 10, 1921, but that the execution was stayed [stopped] by proceedings in Court; we presume the proceedings before the Chancellor to which we shall advert.

In *Frank v. Mangum*, it was recognized of course that if in fact a trial is dominated by a mob so that there is an actual interference with the course of justice, there is a departure from due process of law; and that "if the State, supplying no corrective process, carries into execution a judgment of death or imprisonment based upon a verdict thus produced by mob domination, the State deprives the accused of his life or liberty without due process of law." We assume in accordance with that case that the corrective process supplied by the State may be so adequate that interference by *habeas corpus* [an order to bring someone before the court] ought not to be allowed. It certainly is true that mere mistakes of law in the course of a trial are not to be corrected in that way. But if the case is that the whole proceeding is a mask - that counsel, jury and judge were swept to the fatal end by an irresistible wave of public passion, and that the State Courts failed to correct the wrong, neither perfection in the machinery for correction nor the possibility that the trial court and counsel saw no other way of avoiding an immediate outbreak of the mob can prevent this Court from securing to the petitioners their constitutional rights.

In this case a motion for a new trial on the ground alleged in this petition was overruled and upon . . . appeal to the Supreme Court the judgment was affirmed [upheld]. The Supreme Court said that the complaint of discrimination against petitioners by the exclusion of colored men from the jury came too late and by way of answer to the objection that no fair trial could be had in the circumstances, stated that it could not say "that this must necessarily have been the case"; that eminent counsel was appointed to defend the petitioners, that the trial was had according to law, the jury correctly charged, and the testimony legally sufficient. On June 8, 1921, two days before the date fixed for their execution, a petition for *habeas corpus* was presented to the Chancellor and he issued the writ [court order] and an injunction [an order stopping an action] against the execution of the petitioners; but the Supreme Court of the State held that the Chancellor had no jurisdiction under the state law whatever might be the law of the United States. The present petition perhaps was suggested by the language of the Court: "What the result would be of an application to a Federal Court we need not inquire." It was presented to the District Court on September 21. We shall not say more concerning the corrective process afforded to the petitioners than that it does not seem to us sufficient to allow a Judge of the United States to escape the duty of examining the facts for himself when if true as alleged they make the trial absolutely void. . . . [I]t appears to us unavoidable that the District Judge should find whether the facts alleged are true and whether they can be explained so far as to leave the state proceedings undisturbed.

Order reversed. The case to stand for hearing before the District Court.

MOB JUSTICE

The Scottsboro Boys

On the night of March 25, 1931, on a freight train passing through northeastern Alabama, a fight broke out between two groups of teenage hitchhikers, an unknown number of "negro boys" and nine whites, seven males and two females. In the fight six of the white males and an unknown number of the negroes either jumped off or were thrown off the train. A sheriff's posse, sent to investigate, arrested those remaining and took them to the Jackson County Jail in Scottsboro, Alabama. There the two white females involved in the fight told the sheriff they had been raped by "negro boys." Clarence Norris, Olen Montgomery, Ozie Powell, Haywood Patterson, Willie Roberson, Charlie Weems, Eugene Williams, and Roy and Andy Wright (all nineteen years of age or under, all illiterate, and all from out of state) were charged with rape, a crime punishable by death. On April 1 each of the "Scottsboro Boys" pled not guilty. None were represented by counsel, or asked if they were able to employ counsel, or asked if they wished to have counsel appointed, or given the opportunity to contact family who could obtain counsel for them. Less then a week later, on April 6, with an angry mob of ten thousand surrounding the Jackson County Courthouse and the Alabama National Guard called out to maintain order, the "Scottsboro Boys" went on trial for rape. Their trials lasted one day. Two lawyers, appointed on that day to defend them, put up a minimal defense. The Scottsboro Boys, tried in a hostile environment by an all-white jury, without competent counsel, were found guilty and sentenced by Jackson County Judge Alfred E. Hawkins, to die on July 10 in the electric chair. The Alabama Supreme Court affirmed the death sentences. The Scottsboro Boys appealed to the U.S. Supreme Court.

On November 7, 1932 Justice George Sutherland announced the Court's 7-2 decision. The edited text follows.

THE SCOTTSBORO COURT

Chief Justice Charles Evans Hughes
Appointed by President Hoover
Served 1930 - 1941

Associate Justice Willis Van Devanter
Appointed by President Taft
Served 1910 - 1937

Associate Justice James McReynolds
Appointed by President Wilson
Served 1914 - 1941

Associate Justice Louis Brandeis
Appointed by President Wilson
Served 1916 - 1939

Associate Justice George Sutherland
Appointed by President Harding
Served 1922 - 1938

Associate Justice Pierce Butler
Appointed by President Harding
Served 1922 - 1939

Associate Justice Harlan Fiske Stone
Appointed by President Coolidge
Served 1925 - 1946

Associate Justice Owen Roberts
Appointed by President Hoover
Served 1930 - 1945

Associate Justice Benjamin Cardozo
Appointed by President Hoover
Served 1932 - 1938

The unedited text of *The Scottsboro Boys* can be found on page 45, volume 287 of *United States Reports.*

SCOTTSBORO BOYS v. ALABAMA
November 7, 1932

JUSTICE GEORGE SUTHERLAND: . . . . The petitioners [Ozie Powell, Willie Roberson, Andy Wright, Olen
Montgomery, Haywood Patterson, Charley Weems, and
Clarence Norris], hereinafter referred to as defendants,
are negroes charged with the crime of rape, committed
upon the persons of two white girls. The crime is said to
have been committed on March 25, 1931. The indictment
[charge] was returned in a state court . . . on March 31,
and the record recites that on the same day the defendants
were arraigned [brought before the court] and entered
pleas of not guilty. There is a further recital to the effect
that upon the arraignment they were represented by counsel. But no counsel had been employed, and aside from a
statement made by the trial judge several days later during a [discussion] immediately preceding the trial, the record does not disclose when, or under what circumstances,
an appointment of counsel was made, or who was appointed. . . . [T]he trial judge, in response to a question, said
that he had appointed all the members of the bar for the
purpose of arraigning the defendants and then of course
anticipated that the members of the bar would continue to
help the defendants if no counsel appeared. Upon the argument here both sides accepted that as a correct statement of the facts concerning the matter.

. . . . [T]he defendants were tried in three [separate]
groups. . . . As each of the three cases was called for trial,
each defendant was arraigned, and, having the indictment
read to him, entered a plea of not guilty. Whether the
original arraignment and pleas were regarded as ineffective is not shown. Each of the three trials was completed
within a single day. Under the Alabama statute the pun-

ishment for rape is to be fixed by the jury, and in its discretion may be from ten years' imprisonment to death.
The juries found defendants guilty and imposed the death
penalty upon all. The trial court overruled motions for
new trials and sentenced the defendants in accordance
with the verdicts. The judgments were affirmed [upheld]
by the state supreme court. Chief Justice Anderson
thought the defendants had not been accorded a fair trial
and strongly dissented.

In this court the judgments are assailed upon the grounds
that the defendants . . . were denied due process of law
and the equal protection of the laws, in [violation] of the
Fourteenth Amendment, specifically as follows: (1) they
were not given a fair, impartial and deliberate trial; (2)
they were denied the right of counsel, with the accustomed incidents of consultation and opportunity of preparation for trial; and (3) they were tried before juries from
which qualified members of their own race were systematically excluded. . . .

The only one of the assignments which we shall consider
is the second, in respect of the denial of counsel. . . .

The record shows that on the day when the offense is said
to have been committed, these defendants, together with a
number of other negroes, were upon a freight train on its
way through Alabama. On the same train were seven
white boys and the two white girls. A fight took place between the negroes and the white boys, in the course of
which the white boys, with the exception of one named
Gilley, were thrown off the train. A message was sent
ahead, reporting the fight and asking that every negro be
gotten off the train. The participants in the fight, and the
two girls, were in an open gondola car. The two girls tes-

tified that each of them was assaulted by six different negroes in turn, and they identified the seven defendants as having been among the number. None of the white boys was called to testify, with the exception of Gilley, who was called in rebuttal [an attempt to produce evidence to the contrary].

Before the train reached Scottsboro, Alabama, a sheriff's posse seized the defendants and two other negroes. Both girls and the negroes then were taken to Scottsboro, the county seat. Word of their coming and of the alleged assault had preceded them, and they were met at Scottsboro by a large crowd. It does not sufficiently appear that the defendants were seriously threatened with, or that they were actually in danger of, mob violence; but it does appear that the attitude of the community was one of great hostility. The sheriff thought it necessary to call for the militia to assist in safeguarding the prisoners. Chief Justice Anderson pointed out in his opinion that every step taken from the arrest and arraignment to the sentence was accompanied by the military. Soldiers took the defendants to Gadsden for safekeeping, brought them back to Scottsboro for arraignment, returned them to Gadsden for safekeeping while awaiting trial, escorted them to Scottsboro for trial a few days later, and guarded the court house and grounds at every stage of the proceedings. It is perfectly apparent that the proceedings, from beginning to end, took place in an atmosphere of tense, hostile and excited public sentiment. During the entire time, the defendants were closely confined or were under military guard. The record does not disclose their ages, except that one of them was nineteen; but the record clearly indicates that most, if not all, of them were youthful, and they are constantly referred to as "the boys." They were ignorant and illiterate. All of them were residents of other states, where alone members of their families or friends resided.

However guilty [the] defendants, upon due inquiry might prove to have been, they were, until convicted, presumed to be innocent. It was the duty of the court having their cases in charge to see that they were denied no necessary incident of a fair trial. . . . The sole inquiry which we are permitted to make is whether the federal Constitution was [violated]; and as to that, we confine ourselves, as already suggested to the inquiry whether the defendants were in substance denied the right of counsel, and if so, whether such denial infringes the due process clause of the Fourteenth Amendment.

First. The record shows that immediately upon the return of the indictment defendants were arraigned and pleaded not guilty. Apparently they were not asked whether they had, or were able to employ, counsel, or wished to have counsel appointed; or whether they had friends or relatives who might assist in that regard if communicated with. That it would not have been an idle ceremony to have given the defendants reasonable opportunity to communicate with their families and endeavor to obtain counsel is demonstrated by the fact that very soon after conviction able counsel appeared in their behalf. This was pointed out by Chief Justice Anderson in the course of his dissenting opinion. "They were nonresidents," he said, "and had little time or opportunity to get in touch with their families and friends who were scattered throughout two other states, and time has demonstrated that they could or would have been represented by able counsel had a better opportunity been given by a reasonable delay in the trial of the cases judging from the number and activity of counsel that appeared immediately or shortly after their conviction."

It is hardly necessary to say that the right to counsel being conceded, a defendant should be afforded a fair opportunity to secure counsel of his own choice. Not only was that not done here, but such designation of counsel as was attempted was either so indefinite or so close upon the trial as to amount to a denial of effective and substantial aid in that regard. This will be amply demonstrated by a brief review of the record.

April 6, six days after indictment, the trials began. When the first case was called, the court inquired whether the parties were ready for trial. The state's attorney replied that he was ready to proceed. No one answered for the defendants or appeared to represent or defend them. Mr. Roddy, a Tennessee lawyer not a member of the local bar, addressed the court, saying that he had not been employed, but that people who were interested had spoken to him about the case. He was asked by the court whether he intended to appear for the defendants, and answered that he would like to appear along with counsel that the court might appoint.

. . . . [I]n this casual fashion the matter of counsel in a capital case [one in which the death penalty may be imposed] was disposed of.

It thus will be seen that until the very morning of the trial no lawyer had been named or definitely designated to represent the defendants. Prior to that time, the trial judge had "appointed all the members of the bar" for the limited "purpose of arraigning the defendants." Whether they would represent the defendants thereafter if no counsel appeared in their behalf, was a matter of speculation only, or, as the judge indicated, of mere anticipation on the part of the court. Such a designation, even if made for all purposes, would, in our opinion, have fallen far short of meeting, in any proper sense, a requirement for the appointment of counsel. How many lawyers were members of the bar does not appear; but, in the very nature of things, whether many or few, they would not, thus collectively named, have been given that clear appreciation of responsibility or impressed with that individual sense of duty which should and naturally would accompany the appointment of a selected member of the bar, specifically named and assigned.

That this action of the trial judge in respect of appointment of counsel was little more than an expansive gesture, imposing no substantial or definite obligation upon any one, is borne out by the fact that prior to the calling of the case for trial on April 6, a leading member of the local bar accepted employment on the side of the prosecution and actively participated in the trial. It is true that he said that before doing so he had understood Mr. Roddy would be employed as counsel for the defendants. This the lawyer in question, of his own accord, frankly stated to the court; and no doubt he acted with the utmost good faith. Probably other members of the bar had a like understanding. In any event, the circumstance lends emphasis to the conclusion that during perhaps the most critical period of the proceedings against these defendants, that is to say, from the time of their arraignment until the beginning of their trial, when consultation, thorough-going investigation and preparation were vitally important, the defendants did not have the aid of counsel in any real sense, although they were as much entitled to such aid during that period as at the trial itself.

Nor do we think the situation was helped by what occurred on the morning of the trial. At that time . . . Mr.
Roddy stated to the court that he did not appear as counsel, but that he would like to appear along with counsel
that the court might appoint; that he had not been given
an opportunity to prepare the case; that he was not familiar with the procedure in Alabama, but merely came down
as a friend of the people who were interested; that he
thought the boys would be better off if he should step entirely out of the case. Mr. Moody, a member of the local
bar, expressed a willingness to help Mr. Roddy in anything he could do under the circumstances. To this the
court responded, "All right, all the lawyers that will; of
course I would not require a lawyer to appear if - ." And
Mr. Moody continued, "I am willing to do that for him as
a member of the bar; I will go ahead and help do anything
I can do." With this dubious understanding, the trials immediately proceeded. The defendants, young, ignorant, illiterate, surrounded by hostile sentiment, haled back and
forth under guard of soldiers, charged with an atrocious
crime regarded with especial horror in the community
where they were to be tried, were thus put in peril of
their lives within a few moments after counsel for the
first time charged with any degree of responsibility began
to represent them.

It is not enough to assume that counsel thus precipitated
into the case thought there was no defense, and exercised
their best judgment in proceeding to trial without preparation. Neither they nor the court could say what a
prompt and thorough-going investigation might disclose as
to the facts. No attempt was made to investigate. No opportunity to do so was given. Defendants were immediately hurried to trial. Chief Justice Anderson, after dis-
claiming any intention to criticize harshly counsel who at-

tempted to represent defendants at the trials, said: "The record indicates that the appearance was rather pro forma [routine] than zealous and active." Under the circumstances disclosed, we hold that defendants were not accorded the right of counsel in any substantial sense. To decide otherwise, would simply be to ignore actualities. . . .

It is true that great and inexcusable delay in the enforcement of our criminal law is one of the grave evils of our time. Continuances [postponements] are frequently granted for unnecessarily long periods of time, and delays [for] . . . motions [requests] for new trial and hearings upon appeal have come in many cases to be a distinct reproach to the administration of justice. The prompt disposition of criminal cases is to be commended and encouraged. But in reaching that result a defendant, charged with a serious crime, must not be stripped of his right to have sufficient time to advise with counsel and prepare his defense. To do that is not to proceed promptly in the calm spirit of regulated justice but to go forward with the haste of the mob.

As the court said in *Com. v. O'Keefe*,

> "It is vain to give the accused a day in court, with no opportunity to prepare for it, or to guarantee him counsel without giving the latter any opportunity to acquaint himself with the facts or law of the case."·

[And in *Reliford v. State*]

> "A prompt and vigorous administration of the criminal law is commendable and we have no de-

sire to clog the wheels of justice. What we here
decide is that to force a defendant, charged with
a serious misdemeanor, to trial within five hours
of his arrest, is not due process of law, regardless
of the merits of the case."

Second. The Constitution of Alabama provides that in all
criminal prosecutions the accused shall enjoy the right to
have the assistance of counsel; and a state statute requires
the court in a capital case, where the defendant is unable
to employ counsel, to appoint counsel for him. The state
supreme court held that these provisions had not been infringed, and with that holding we are powerless to interfere. The question, however, which it is our duty, and
within our power, to decide, is whether the denial of the
assistance of counsel [violates] the due process clause of
the Fourteenth Amendment to the federal Constitution.

.... [H]ow can a judge, whose functions are purely judicial, effectively discharge the obligations of counsel for
the accused? He can and should see to it that in the proceedings before the court the accused shall be dealt with
justly and fairly. He cannot investigate the facts, advise
and direct the defense, or participate in those necessary
conferences between counsel and accused which sometimes partake of the inviolable character of the confes-
sional.

.... It ... appears that in at least twelve of the thirteen
colonies ... the right to counsel [was] fully recognized in
all criminal prosecutions, save that in one or two instances
the right was limited to capital offenses or to the more serious crimes. ...

The Sixth Amendment . . . provides that in all criminal prosecutions the accused shall enjoy the right "to have the assistance of counsel for his defense."

. . . . [T]his court has considered that freedom of speech and of the press are rights protected by the due process clause of the Fourteenth Amendment, although in the First Amendment, Congress is prohibited in specific terms from abridging the right.

. . . . The rule is an aid to construction, and in some instances may be conclusive; but it must yield to more compelling considerations whenever such considerations exist. The fact that the right involved is of such a character that it cannot be denied without violating those "fundamental principles of liberty and justice which lie at the base of all our civil and political institutions" is obviously one of those compelling considerations which must prevail in determining whether it is embraced within the due process clause of the Fourteenth Amendment, although it be specifically dealt with in another part of the federal Constitution. . . . [I]n *Twining v. New Jersey*, Justice Moody, speaking for the court, said that " . . . it is possible that some of the personal rights safeguarded by the first eight Amendments against national action may also be safeguarded against state action, because a denial of them would be a denial of due process of law. If this is so, it is not because those rights are enumerated in the first eight Amendments, but because they are of such a nature that they are included in the conception of due process of law." While the question has never been categorically determined by this court, a consideration of the nature of the right and a review of the expressions of this and other courts, make it clear that the right to the aid of counsel is of this fundamental character.

It never has been doubted by this court, or any other so far as we know, that notice and hearing are preliminary steps essential to the passing of an enforceable judgment, and that they, together with a legally competent tribunal having jurisdiction of the case, constitute basic elements of the constitutional requirement of due process of law. The words of Webster, so often quoted, that by "the law of the land" is intended "a law which hears before it condemns," have been repeated in varying forms of expression in a multitude of decisions. . . .

Justice Field, in . . . *Galpin v. Page*, said that the rule that no one shall be personally bound until he has had his day in court was as old as the law, and it meant that he must be cited [summoned] to appear and afforded an opportunity to be heard. . . .

What, then, does a hearing include? Historically and in practice, in our own country at least, it has always included the right to the aid of counsel when desired and provided by the party asserting the right. The right to be heard would be, in many cases, of little avail if it did not comprehend the right to be heard by counsel. Even the intelligent and educated layman has small and sometimes no skill in the science of law. If charged with crime, he is incapable, generally, of determining for himself whether the indictment is good or bad. . . . Left without the aid of counsel he may be put on trial without a proper charge, and convicted upon incompetent evidence, or evidence irrelevant to the issue or otherwise inadmissible. He lacks both the skill and knowledge adequately to prepare his defense, even though he have a perfect one. He requires the guiding hand of counsel at every step in the proceedings against him. Without it, though he be not guilty, he faces the danger of conviction because he does not know how to establish his innocence. If that be true of men of intelligence, how much more true is it of the ignorant and illiterate, or those of feeble intellect. If in any case, civil or criminal, a state or federal court were arbitrarily to refuse to hear a party by counsel, employed by and appearing for him, it reasonably may not be doubted that such a refusal would be a denial of a hearing, and, therefore, of due process in the constitutional sense.

. . . . In the light of the facts outlined in the forepart of this opinion - the ignorance and illiteracy of the defendants, their youth, the circumstances of public hostility, the imprisonment and the close surveillance of the defendants by the military forces, the fact that their friends and families were all in other states and communication with them necessarily difficult, and above all that they stood in deadly peril of their lives - we think the failure of the trial court to give them reasonable time and opportunity to secure counsel was a clear denial of due process.

But passing that, and assuming their inability, even if opportunity had been given, to employ counsel, as the trial court evidently did assume, we are of opinion that, under the circumstances just stated, the necessity of counsel was so vital and imperative that the failure of the trial court to make an effective appointment of counsel was likewise a denial of due process within the meaning of the Fourteenth Amendment. Whether this would be so in other criminal prosecutions, or under other circumstances, we need not determine. All that it is necessary now to decide, as we do decide, is that in a capital case, where the defendant is unable to employ counsel, and is incapable adequately of making his own defense because of ignorance, feeblemindedness, illiteracy, or the like, it is the duty of the court, whether requested or not, to assign counsel for

him as a necessary requisite of due process of law; and
that duty is not discharged by an assignment at such a
time or under such circumstances as to preclude the giving of effective aid in the preparation and trial of the
case. To hold otherwise would be to ignore the fundamental [proposition] "that there are certain immutable
principles of justice which inhere in the very idea of free
government which no member of the Union may disregard." In a case such as this, whatever may be the rule in
other cases, the right to have counsel appointed, when necessary, [logically follows] from the constitutional right to
be heard by counsel.

In *Hendryx v. State*, there was no statute authorizing the
assignment of an attorney to defend an indigent person
accused of crime, but the court held that such an assignment was necessary to accomplish the ends of public justice, and that the court possessed the inherent power to
make it. "Where a prisoner," the court said, "without legal
knowledge, is confined in jail, absent from his friends,
without the aid of legal advice or the means of investigat-
ing the charge against him, it is impossible to conceive of
a fair trial where he is compelled to conduct his cause in
court, without the aid of counsel. . . .

Let us suppose the extreme case of a prisoner charged
with a capital offense, who is deaf and dumb, illiterate
and feeble-minded, unable to employ counsel, with the
whole power of the state arrayed against him, prosecuted
by counsel for the state without assignment of counsel for
his defense, tried, convicted and sentenced to death. Such
a result, which, if carried into execution, would be little
short of judicial murder, it cannot be doubted would be a
gross violation of the guaranty of due process of law; and
we venture to think that no appellate court, state or feder-

al, would hesitate so to decide. The duty of the trial court to appoint counsel under such circumstances is clear, as it is clear under circumstances such as are disclosed by the record here; and its power to do so, even in the absence of a statute, can not be questioned. Attorneys are officers of the court, and are bound to render service when required by such an appointment.

The United States by statute and every state in the Union by express provision of law, or by the determination of its courts, make it the duty of the trial judge, where the accused is unable to employ counsel, to appoint counsel for him. In most states the rule applies broadly to all criminal prosecutions, in others it is limited to the more serious crimes, and in a very limited number, to capital cases. A rule adopted with such unanimous accord reflects, if it does not establish the inherent right to have counsel appointed at least in cases like the present, and lends convincing support to the conclusion we have reached as to the fundamental nature of that right.

The judgments must be reversed and the causes remanded [returned to the lower court] for further proceedings not inconsistent with this opinion.

Clarence Norris, the last surviving Scottsboro Boy, was pardoned in October 1976 by Alabama Governor George C. Wallace.

SCHOOL DESEGREGATION

Brown v. Board of Education I

The doctrine of Separate But Equal was established by the U.S. Supreme Court in the 1896 case of *Plessy v. Ferguson.* The *Plessy* decision said that equality of treatment was achieved when races were provided substantially separate but equal facilities. *Plessy* severely limited the Fourteenth Amendment's Equal Protection Clause and by the early 1950's this still allowed twenty-one states plus the District of Columbia to maintain segregated public schools. In 1952 the NAACP's Legal Defense and Education Fund, headed by civil rights lawyer Thurgood Marshall, challenged the Supreme Court to overrule *Plessy.* Four school desegregation cases were accepted for review: *Briggs* from Clarendon County, South Carolina; *Davis* from Prince Edward County, Virginia; *Gebhart* from the State of Delaware; and *Brown* from Topeka, Kansas.

In 1951 eight-year-old Linda Brown, called by the Court a "minor of the Negro race," was attending an all-black public school in Topeka, Kansas. Linda's school, 21 blocks from her home, was in every way inferior to the all-white public school only five blocks away. Oliver Brown, her father, and the parents of twelve other black schoolchildren, sued the Topeka Board of Education in U.S. District Court to admit Linda and the others to the local all-white school. The NAACP's Legal Defense and Education Fund, which represented Linda, based their argument for the reversal of *Plessy* on the Fourteenth Amendment's Equal Protection Clause, which says: *No state shall make or enforce any law which shall deny any person within its jurisdiction the equal protection of the laws.* The District Court denied Linda admission to the white school. The Browns appealed to the U.S. Supreme Court.

On May 17, 1954 Chief Justice Earl Warren announced the 9-0 decision of the Court. The edited text follows.

THE BROWN I COURT

Chief Justice Earl Warren
Appointed by President Eisenhower
Served 1953 - 1969

Associate Justice Hugo Black
Appointed by President Franklin Roosevelt
Served 1937 - 1971

Associate Justice Stanley Reed
Appointed by President Franklin Roosevelt
Served 1938 - 1957

Associate Justice Felix Frankfurter
Appointed by President Franklin Roosevelt
Served 1939 - 1962

Associate Justice William O. Douglas
Appointed by President Franklin Roosevelt
Served 1939 - 1975

Associate Justice Robert Jackson
Appointed by President Franklin Roosevelt
Served 1941 - 1954

Associate Justice Harold Burton
Appointed by President Truman
Served 1945 - 1958

Associate Justice Tom Clark
Appointed by President Truman
Served 1949 - 1967

Associate Justice Sherman Minton
Appointed by President Truman
Served 1949 - 1956

The unedited text of *Brown v. Board of Education I* is found on page 483, volume 347 of *United States Reports*.

BROWN v. BOARD OF EDUCATION I
May 17, 1954

CHIEF JUSTICE EARL WARREN: These cases come to us from the States of Kansas, South Carolina, Virginia, and Delaware. They are premised on different facts and different local conditions, but a common legal question justifies their consideration together in this consolidated opinion.

In each of the cases, minors of the Negro race [called the plaintiffs], through their legal representatives, seek the aid of the courts in obtaining admission to the public schools of their community on a nonsegregated basis. In each instance, they had been denied admission to schools attended by white children under laws requiring or permitting segregation according to race. This segregation was alleged to deprive the plaintiffs of the equal protection of the laws under the Fourteenth Amendment. In each of the cases other than the Delaware case, a three-judge federal district court denied relief to the plaintiffs on the so-called "separate but equal" doctrine announced by this Court in [the 1896 decision] *Plessy v. Ferguson.* Under that doctrine, equality of treatment is accorded when the races are provided substantially equal facilities, even though these facilities be separate. In the Delaware case, the Supreme Court of Delaware adhered to that doctrine, but ordered that the plaintiffs be admitted to the white schools because of their superiority to the Negro schools.

The plaintiffs contend that segregated public schools are not "equal" and cannot be made "equal," and that hence they are deprived of the equal protection of the laws. Because of the obvious importance of the question presented, the Court [agreed to hear the case]. Argument was heard in the 1952 Term, and reargument was heard this Term on certain questions [asked] by the Court.

Reargument was largely devoted to the circumstances surrounding the adoption of the Fourteenth Amendment in 1868. It covered exhaustively consideration of the Amendment in Congress, ratification by the states, then existing practices in racial segregation, and the views of proponents and opponents of the Amendment. This discussion and our own investigation convince us that, although these sources cast some light, it is not enough to resolve the problem with which we are faced. At best, they are inconclusive. The most avid proponents of the post-[Civil] War Amendments undoubtedly intended them to remove all legal distinctions among "all persons born or naturalized in the United States." Their opponents, just as certainly, were antagonistic to both the letter and the spirit of the Amendments and wished them to have the most limited effect. What others in Congress and the state legislatures had in mind cannot be determined with any degree of certainty.

An additional reason for the inconclusive nature of the Amendment's history, with respect to segregated schools, is the status of public education at that time. In the South, the movement toward free common schools, supported by general taxation, had not yet taken hold. Education of white children was largely in the hands of private groups. Education of Negroes was almost nonexistent, and practically all of the race were illiterate. In fact, any education of Negroes was forbidden by law in some states. Today, in contrast, many Negroes have achieved outstanding success in the arts and sciences as well as in the business and professional world. It is true that public school education at the time of the Amendment had advanced further in the North, but the effect of the Amendment on Northern States was generally ignored in the Congressional debates. Even in the North, the conditions of public education did not approximate those existing today. The curriculum was usually rudimentary; ungraded schools were common in rural areas; the school term was but three months a year in many states; and compulsory school attendance was virtually unknown. As a consequence, it is not surprising that there should be so little in the history of the Fourteenth Amendment relating to its intended effect on public education.

In the first cases in this Court construing [interpreting] the Fourteenth Amendment, decided shortly after its adoption, the Court interpreted it as [prohibiting] all state-imposed discriminations against the Negro race. The doctrine of "separate but equal" did not make its appearance in this Court until 1896 in the case of *Plessy v. Ferguson*, involving not education but transportation. American courts have since labored with the doctrine for over half a century. In this Court, there have been six cases involving the "separate but equal" doctrine in the field of public education. In *Cumming v. County Board of Education*, and *Gong Lum v. Rice*, the validity of the doctrine itself was not challenged. In more recent cases, all on the graduate school level, inequality was found in that specific benefits enjoyed by white students were denied to Negro students of the same educational qualifications. In none of these cases was it necessary to re-examine the doctrine to grant relief to the Negro plaintiff. And in *Sweatt v. Painter*, the Court expressly reserved decision on the question whether *Plessy v. Ferguson* should be held inapplicable to public education.

In [these] cases, that question is directly presented. Here, unlike *Sweatt v. Painter*, there are findings [in lower State and Federal Courts] that the Negro and white schools involved have been equalized, or are being equalized, with respect to buildings, curricula, qualifications and salaries of teachers, and other "tangible" factors. Our decision, therefore, cannot turn on merely a comparison of these tangible factors in the Negro and white schools involved in each of the cases. We must look instead to the effect of segregation itself on public education.

In approaching this problem, we cannot turn the clock back to 1868 when the Amendment was adopted, or even to 1896 when *Plessy v. Ferguson* was written.

We must consider public education in the light of its full development and its present place in American life throughout the Nation. Only in this way can it be determined if segregation in public schools deprives these plaintiffs of the equal protection of the laws.

Today, education is perhaps the most important function of state and local governments. Compulsory school attendance laws and the great expenditures for education both demonstrate our recognition of the importance of education to our democratic society. It is required in the performance of our most basic public responsibilities, even service in the armed forces. It is the very foundation of good citizenship. Today it is a principal instrument in awakening the child to cultural values, in preparing him for later professional training, and in helping him to adjust normally to his environment. In these days, it is doubtful that any child may reasonably be expected to succeed in life if he is denied the opportunity of an education. Such an opportunity, where the state has undertaken to provide it, is a right which must be made available to all on equal terms.

We come then to the question presented: Does segregation of children in public schools solely on the basis of race, even though the physical facilities and other "tangible" factors may be equal, deprive the children of the minority group of equal educational opportunities? We believe that it does.

In *Sweatt v. Painter*, in finding that a segregated law school for Negroes could not provide them equal educational opportunities, this Court relied in large part on "those qualities which are incapable of objective measurement but which make for greatness in a law school." In *McLaurin v. Oklahoma State Regents*, the Court, in requiring that a Negro admitted to a white graduate school be treated like all other students, again resorted to intangible considerations: ". . . his ability to study, to engage in discussions and exchange views with other students, and, in general, to learn his profession." Such considerations apply with added force to children in grade and high schools. To separate them from others of similar age and qualifications solely because of their race generates a feeling of inferiority as to their status in the community that may affect their hearts and minds in a way unlikely ever to be undone. The effect of this separation on their educational opportunities was well stated by a finding in the Kansas case by a court which nevertheless felt compelled to rule against the Negro plaintiffs:

"Segregation of white and colored children in public schools has a detrimental effect upon the colored children. The impact is greater when it has the sanction of the law; for the policy of separating the races is usually interpreted as denoting the inferiority of the negro group. A sense of inferiority affects the motivation of a child to learn. Segregation with the sanction of law, therefore, has a tendency to [retard] the educational and mental development of negro children and to deprive them of some of the benefits they would receive in a racial[ly] integrated school system."

Whatever may have been the extent of psychological knowledge at the time of *Plessy v. Ferguson,* this finding is amply supported by modern authority. Any language in *Plessy v. Ferguson* contrary to this finding is rejected.

We conclude that in the field of public education the doctrine of "separate but equal" has no place. Separate educational facilities are inherently unequal. Therefore, we hold that the plaintiffs and others similarly situated for whom the actions have been brought are, by reason of the segregation complained of, deprived of the equal protection of the laws guaranteed by the Fourteenth Amendment. This disposition makes unnecessary any discussion whether such segregation also violates the Due Process Clause of the Fourteenth Amendment.

Because these are class actions [where one person represents a larger group], because of the wide applicability of this decision, and because of the great variety of local conditions, the formulation of decrees [orders of the court] in these cases presents problems of considerable complexity. On reargument, the consideration of appropriate relief [how to end school segregation] was necessarily subordinated to the primary question - the constitutionality of segregation in public education. We have now announced that such segregation is a denial of the equal protection of the laws. In order that we may have the full assistance of the parties in formulating decrees, the cases will be restored to the docket [put on the Court's calendar], and the parties are requested to present further argument on [these issues] for the reargument this Term. The Attorney General of the United States is again invited to participate. The Attorneys General of the states requiring or permitting segregation in public education will also be permitted to appear as *amici curiae* [friends of the Court] upon request to do so by September 15, 1954, and submission of briefs by October 1, 1954. It is so ordered.

SCHOOL DESEGREGATION
Brown v. Board of Education II

We reaffirm our reliance on the Constitution as the fundamental law of the land. We decry the Supreme Court's encroachment on the rights reserved to the states and the people, contrary to established law and to the Constitution. We commend the motives of those states which have declared the intention to resist forced integration by any lawful means. We appeal to the states and people who are not directly affected by these decisions to consider the constitutional principles involved against the time when they too, on issues vital to them, may be the victims of judicial encroachment. . . . We pledge ourselves to use all lawful means to bring about a reversal of this decision which is contrary to the Constitution and to prevent the use of force in its implementation.
The Southern Declaration on Integration

Brown v. Board of Education ignited a storm of public and legal protest. The public education systems of the twenty-one states and the District of Columbia, all of which either required or permitted racial discrimination in public education, were thrown into chaos. The Supreme Court, in order to begin the process of school desegregation in these jurisdictions, ordered the parties directly impacted by *Brown,* the school boards of Topeka, Kansas; Clarendon County, South Carolina; Prince Edward County, Virginia; and the State of Delaware to argue before the Court how the *Brown* decision would be implemented. Participating in the oral arguments held before the Court on April 11-14, 1955 were the parties directly impacted, plus the Attorney General of the United States and the Attorney Generals of six individual states, Florida, North Carolina, Arkansas, Oklahoma, Maryland, and Texas.

On May 31, 1955 Chief Justice Earl Warren announced the 9-0 decision of the Court. The edited text follows.

THE BROWN II COURT

Chief Justice Earl Warren
Appointed by President Eisenhower
Served 1953 - 1969

Associate Justice Hugo Black
Appointed by President Franklin Roosevelt
Served 1937 - 1971

Associate Justice Stanley Reed
Appointed by President Franklin Roosevelt
Served 1938 - 1957

Associate Justice Felix Frankfurter
Appointed by President Franklin Roosevelt
Served 1939 - 1962

Associate Justice William O. Douglas
Appointed by President Franklin Roosevelt
Served 1939 - 1975

Associate Justice Harold Burton
Appointed by President Truman
Served 1945 - 1958

Associate Justice Tom Clark
Appointed by President Truman
Served 1949 - 1967

Associate Justice Sherman Minton
Appointed by President Truman
Served 1949 - 1956

Associate Justice John M. Harlan
Appointed by President Eisenhower
Served 1955 - 1971

The unedited text of *Brown v. Board of Education II* is
found on page 294, volume 349 of *United States Reports.*

BROWN v. BOARD OF EDUCATION II
May 31, 1955

CHIEF JUSTICE WARREN: [This case was] decided on May 17, 1954. The [opinion] of that date, declaring the fundamental principle that racial discrimination in public education is unconstitutional, [is] incorporated herein by reference. All provisions of federal, state, or local law requiring or permitting such discrimination must yield to this principle. There remains for consideration the manner in which relief is to be accorded.

. . . . In view of the nationwide importance of the decision, we invited the Attorney General of the United States and the Attorneys General of all states requiring or permitting racial discrimination in public education to present their views on that question. The parties, the United States, and the States of Florida, North Carolina, Arkansas, Oklahoma, Maryland, and Texas filed briefs and participated in the oral argument.

These presentations were informative and helpful to the Court in its consideration of the complexities arising from the transition to a system of public education freed of racial discrimination. The presentations also demonstrated that substantial steps to eliminate racial discrimination in public schools have already been taken, not only in some of the communities in which these cases arose, but in some of the states appearing as *amici curiae* [friends of the court], and in other states as well. Substantial progress has been made in the District of Columbia and in the communities in Kansas and Delaware involved in this litigation. The defendants in the cases coming to us from South Carolina and Virginia are awaiting the decision of this Court concerning relief.

Full implementation of these constitutional principles may require solution of varied local school problems. School authorities have the primary responsibility for elucidating, assessing, and solving these problems; courts will have to consider whether the action of school authorities constitutes good faith implementation of the governing constitutional principles. Because of their proximity to local conditions and the possible need for further hearings, the courts which originally heard these cases can best perform this judicial appraisal. Accordingly, we believe it appropriate to remand [return] the cases to those courts.

In fashioning and effectuating the decrees, the courts will be guided by equitable principles. Traditionally, equity [fairness] has been characterized by a practical flexibility in shaping its remedies and by a facility for adjusting and reconciling public and private needs. These cases call for the exercise of these traditional attributes of equity power. At stake is the personal interest of the plaintiffs [Brown and the others] in admission to public schools as soon as practicable on a nondiscriminatory basis. To effectuate this interest may call for elimination of a variety of obstacles in making the transition to school systems operated in accordance with the constitutional principles set forth in our May 17, 1954, decision. Courts of equity may properly take into account the public interest in the elimination of such obstacles in a systematic and effective manner. But it should go without saying that the vitality of these constitutional principles cannot be allowed to yield simply because of disagreement with them.

While giving weight to these public and private considerations, the courts will require that the defendants [the Board of Education] make a prompt and reasonable start toward full compliance with our May 17, 1954, ruling.

Once such a start has been made, the courts may find that additional time is necessary to carry out the ruling in an effective manner. The burden rests upon the [School Board] to establish that such time is necessary in the public interest and is consistent with good faith compliance at the earliest practicable date. To that end, the courts may consider problems related to administration, arising from the physical condition of the school plant, the school transportation system, personnel, revision of school districts and attendance areas into compact units to achieve a system of determining admission to the public schools on a nonracial basis, and revision of local laws and regulations which may be necessary in solving the foregoing problems. They will also consider the adequacy of any plans the [School Board] may propose to meet these problems and to effectuate a transition to a racially nondiscriminatory school system. During this period of transition, the courts will retain jurisdiction of these cases.

The [judgment] below . . . [is] accordingly reversed and the [case is] remanded to the District [Court] to take such proceedings and enter such orders and decrees consistent with this opinion as are necessary and proper to admit to public schools on a racially nondiscriminatory basis with all deliberate speed [Brown and the others]. . . . It is so ordered.

THE LITTLE ROCK CRISIS

Cooper v. Aaron

The People of Arkansas assert that the power to operate public schools in the State on a racially separate but substantially equal basis was granted by the people of Arkansas to the government of the State of Arkansas; and that, by ratification of the Fourteenth Amendment, neither the State of Arkansas nor its people delegated to the federal government, expressly or by implication, the power to regulate or control the domestic institutions of Arkansas; any and all decisions of the federal courts or any other department of the federal government to the contrary notwithstanding. **Arkansas Governor Orval E. Faubus**

The Little Rock, Arkansas Independent School District, with the approval of a Federal District Court, planned, on September 3, 1957, to admit nine Negro students to the previously all-white Central High School. On September 2 Governor Orval Faubus ordered the Arkansas National Guard to place the school "off limits" to colored students. On September 25, after three weeks of violent racial strife President Eisenhower, stating that "[m]ob rule cannot be allowed to overrule the decisions of our courts," sent in federal troops to desegregate Central High. The troops stayed for the entire school year. In early 1958 the School Board petitioned the District Court to withdraw the Negro students and postpone desegregation. Thelma Aaron, on behalf of her children, brought suit against William Cooper and the other members of the Little Rock Board. The District Court, finding desegregation had caused "tension, chaos, bedlam and turmoil," approved the postponement and the Court of Appeals reversed it. An appeal was taken to the U.S. Supreme Court.

On September 29, 1958 the Court announced their 9-0 *Per Curiam* [by the Court without attribution of authorship] decision. The edited text follows.

THE COOPER COURT

Chief Justice Earl Warren
Appointed by President Eisenhower
Served 1953 - 1969

Associate Justice Hugo Black
Appointed by President Franklin Roosevelt
Served 1937 - 1971

Associate Justice Felix Frankfurter
Appointed by President Franklin Roosevelt
Served 1939 - 1962

Associate Justice William O. Douglas
Appointed by President Franklin Roosevelt
Served 1939 - 1975

Associate Justice Harold Burton
Appointed by President Truman
Served 1945 - 1958

Associate Justice Tom Clark
Appointed by President Truman
Served 1949 - 1967

Associate Justice John M. Harlan
Appointed by President Eisenhower
Served 1955 - 1971

Associate Justice William Brennan
Appointed by President Eisenhower
Served 1956 - 1990

Associate Justice Charles Whittaker
Appointed by President Eisenhower
Served 1957 - 1962

The unedited text of *Cooper v. Aaron* is found on page 1, volume 358 of *United States Reports.*

COOPER v. AARON
September 29, 1958

PER CURIAM [by the entire Court]: As this case reaches us it raises questions of the highest importance to the maintenance of our federal system of government. It necessarily involves a claim by the Governor and Legislature of a State that there is no duty on state officials to obey federal court orders resting on this Court's considered interpretation of the United States Constitution. Specifically it involves actions by the Governor and Legislature of Arkansas upon the premise that they are not bound by our holding in *Brown v. Board of Education.* That holding was that the Fourteenth Amendment forbids States to use their governmental powers to bar children on racial grounds from attending schools where there is state participation through any arrangement, management, funds or property. We are urged to uphold a suspension of the Little Rock School Board's plan to do away with segregated public schools in Little Rock until state laws and efforts to upset and nullify our holding in *Brown v. Board of Education* have been further challenged and tested in the courts. We reject these contentions.

The case was argued before us on September 11, 1958. On the following day we unanimously affirmed [upheld] the judgment of the Court of Appeals for the Eighth Circuit, which had reversed a judgment of the District Court for the Eastern District of Arkansas. The District Court had granted the application of the petitioners, the Little Rock School Board and School Superintendent, to suspend for two and one-half years the operation of the School Board's court-approved desegregation program. In order that the School Board might know, without doubt, its duty in this regard before the opening of school, which had been set for the following Monday, September 15, 1958, we immediately issued the judgment. . . . This opinion of all of the members of the Court embodies those views.

The following are the facts and circumstances so far as necessary to show how the legal questions are presented.

On May 17, 1954, this Court decided that enforced racial segregation in the public schools of a State is a denial of the equal protection of the laws enjoined [required] by the Fourteenth Amendment. The Court postponed, pending further argument, formulation of a decree to effectuate this decision. That decree was rendered May 31, 1955 [in *Brown II*]. In the formulation of that decree the Court recognized that good faith compliance with the principles declared in *Brown* might in some situations "call for elimination of a variety of obstacles in making the transition to school systems operated in accordance with the constitutional principles set forth in our May 17, 1954, decision." . . .

Under such circumstances, the District Courts were directed to require "a prompt and reasonable start toward full compliance," and to take such action as was necessary to bring about the end of racial segregation in the public schools "with all deliberate speed." Of course, in many locations, obedience to the duty of desegregation would require the immediate general admission of Negro children, otherwise qualified as students for their appropriate classes, at particular schools. On the other hand, a District Court, after analysis of the relevant factors (which, of course, excludes hostility to racial desegregation), might conclude that justification existed for not requiring the present nonsegregated admission of all qualified Negro children. In such circumstances, however, the courts should scrutinize the program of the school authorities to make sure that they had developed arrangements pointed toward the earliest practicable completion of desegregation, and had taken appropriate steps to put their program into effective operation. It was made plain that delay in any guise in order to deny the constitutional rights of Negro children could not be countenanced, and that only a prompt start, diligently and earnestly pursued, to eliminate racial segregation from the public schools could constitute good faith compliance. State authorities were thus duty bound to devote every effort toward initiating desegregation and bringing about the elimination of racial discrimination in the public school system.

On May 20, 1954, three days after the first *Brown* opinion, the Little Rock District School Board adopted, and on May 23, 1954, made public, a statement of policy entitled "Supreme Court Decision - Segregation in Public Schools." In this statement the Board recognized that

"It is our responsibility to comply with Federal Constitutional Requirements and we intend to do so when the Supreme Court of the United States outlines the method to be followed."

Thereafter the Board undertook studies of the administrative problems confronting the transition to a desegregated public school system at Little Rock. It instructed the Superintendent of Schools to prepare a plan for desegregation, and approved such a plan on May 24, 1955, seven days before the second *Brown* opinion. The plan provided for desegregation at the senior high school level (grades 10 through 12) as the first stage. Desegregation at the junior high and elementary levels was to follow. It was contemplated that desegregation at the high school level

would commence in the fall of 1957, and the expectation
was that complete desegregation of the school system
would be accomplished by 1963. Following the adoption
of this plan, the Superintendent of Schools discussed it
with a large number of citizen groups in the city. As a result of these discussions, the Board reached the conclusion
that "a large majority of the residents" of Little Rock
were of "the belief . . . that the Plan, although objectionable in principle," from the point of view of those supporting segregated schools, "was still the best for the interests of all pupils in the District."

Upon challenge by a group of Negro plaintiffs desiring
more rapid completion of the desegregation process, the
District Court upheld the School Board's plan [in] *Aaron
v. Cooper.* The Court of Appeals affirmed. Review of
that judgment was not sought here.

While the School Board was thus going forward with its
preparation for desegregating the Little Rock school system, other state authorities, in contrast, were actively pur-
suing a program designed to perpetuate in Arkansas the
system of racial segregation which this Court had held violated the Fourteenth Amendment. First came, in November 1956, an amendment to the State Constitution flatly
commanding the Arkansas General Assembly to oppose
"in every Constitutional manner the Un-constitutional desegregation decisions of May 17, 1954 and May 31, 1955
of the United States Supreme Court," and, through the ini-
tiative, a pupil assignment law. Pursuant to this state constitutional command, a law relieving school children from
compulsory attendance at racially mixed schools, and a
law establishing a State Sovereignty Commission, were enacted by the General Assembly in February 1957.

The School Board and the Superintendent of Schools nevertheless continued with preparations to carry out the
first stage of the desegregation program. Nine Negro
children were scheduled for admission in September 1957
to Central High School, which has more than two thousand students. Various administrative measures, designed
to assure the smooth transition of this first stage of desegregation, were undertaken.

On September 2, 1957, the day before these Negro students were to enter Central High, the school authorities
were met with drastic opposing action on the part of the
Governor of Arkansas who dispatched units of the Arkansas National Guard to the Central High School grounds
and placed the school "off limits" to colored students. As
found by the District Court in subsequent proceedings,
the Governor's action had not been requested by the
school authorities, and was entirely unheralded. The findings were these:

> "Up to this time [September 2], no crowds had
> gathered about Central High School and no acts
> of violence or threats of violence in connection
> with the carrying out of the plan had occurred.
> Nevertheless, out of an abundance of caution, the
> school authorities had frequently conferred with
> the Mayor and Chief of Police of Little Rock
> about taking appropriate steps by the Little Rock
> police to prevent any possible disturbances or acts
> of violence in connection with the attendance of
> the 9 colored students at Central High School.
> The Mayor considered that the Little Rock police
> force could adequately cope with any incidents
> which might arise at the opening of school. The
> Mayor, the Chief of Police, and the school au-

thorities made no request to the Governor or any representative of his for State assistance in maintaining peace and order at Central High School. Neither the Governor nor any other official of the State government consulted with the Little Rock authorities about whether the Little Rock police were prepared to cope with any incidents which might arise at the school, about any need for State assistance in maintaining peace and order, or about stationing the Arkansas National Guard at Central High School."

The Board's petition for postponement in this proceeding states: "The effect of that action [of the Governor] was to harden the core of opposition to the Plan and cause many persons who theretofore had reluctantly accepted the Plan to believe there was some power in the State of Arkansas which, when exerted, could nullify the Federal law and permit disobedience of the decree of this [District] Court, and from that date hostility to the Plan was increased and criticism of the officials of the [School] District has become more bitter and unrestrained." The Governor's action caused the School Board to request the Negro students on September 2 not to attend the high school "until the legal dilemma was solved." The next day, September 3, 1957, the Board petitioned the District Court for instructions and the court, after a hearing, found that the Board's request of the Negro students to stay away from the high school had been made because of the stationing of the military guards by the state authorities. The court determined that this was not a reason for departing from the approved plan, and ordered the School Board and Superintendent to proceed with it.

On the morning of the next day, September 4, 1957, the Negro children attempted to enter the high school but, as the District Court later found, units of the Arkansas National Guard "acting pursuant to the Governor's order, stood shoulder to shoulder at the school grounds and thereby forcibly prevented the 9 Negro students . . . from entering," as they continued to do every school day during the following three weeks.

That same day, September 4, 1957, the United States Attorney for the Eastern District of Arkansas was requested by the District Court to begin an immediate investigation in order to fix responsibility for the interference with the orderly implementation of the District Court's direction to carry out the desegregation program. Three days later, September 7, the District Court denied a petition of the School Board and the Superintendent of Schools for an order temporarily suspending continuance of the program.

Upon completion of the United States Attorney's investigation, he and the Attorney General of the United States, at the District Court's request, entered the proceedings and filed a petition on behalf of the United States, as *amicus curiae* [a friend of the Court], to enjoin [stop] the Governor of Arkansas and officers of the Arkansas National Guard from further attempts to prevent obedience to the court's order. After hearings on the petition, the District Court found that the School Board's plan had been obstructed by the Governor through the use of National Guard troops, and granted a preliminary injunction [a court order stopping an act] on September 20, 1957, enjoining the Governor and the officers of the Guard from preventing the attendance of Negro children at Central High School, and from otherwise obstructing or interfering with the orders of the court in connection with the

plan. The National Guard was then withdrawn from the
school.

The next school day was Monday, September 23, 1957.
The Negro children entered the high school that morning
under the protection of the Little Rock Police Department and members of the Arkansas State Police. But the
officers caused the children to be removed from the
school during the morning because they had difficulty
controlling a large and demonstrating crowd which had
gathered at the high school. On September 25, however,
the President of the United States dispatched federal
troops to Central High School and admission of the Negro
students to the school was thereby effected. Regular
army troops continued at the high school until November
27, 1957. They were then replaced by federalized National Guardsmen who remained throughout the balance of
the school year. Eight of the Negro students remained in
attendance at the school throughout the school year.

We come now to the aspect of the proceedings presently
before us. On February 20, 1958, the School Board and
the Superintendent of Schools filed a petition in the District Court seeking a postponement of their program for
desegregation. Their position in essence was that because
of extreme public hostility, which they stated had been
engendered largely by the official attitudes and actions of
the Governor and the Legislature, the maintenance of a
sound educational program at Central High School, with
the Negro students in attendance, would be impossible.
The Board therefore proposed that the Negro students already admitted to the schools be withdrawn and sent to
segregated schools, and that all further steps to carry out
the Board's desegregation program be postponed for a pe-

riod later suggested by the Board to be two and one-half
years.

After a hearing the District Court granted the relief requested by the Board. Among other things the court
found that the past year at Central High School had been
attended by conditions of "chaos, bedlam and turmoil";
that there were "repeated incidents of more or less serious
violence directed against the Negro students and their
property"; that there was "tension and unrest among the
school administrators, the class-room teachers, the pupils,
and the latter's parents, which inevitably had an adverse
effect upon the educational program"; that a school official was threatened with violence; that a "serious financial
burden" had been cast on the School District; that the education of the students had suffered "and under existing
conditions will continue to suffer"; that the Board would
continue to need "military assistance or its equivalent";
that the local police department would not be able "to detail enough men to afford the necessary protection"; and
that the situation was "intolerable."

The District Court's judgment was dated June 20, 1958.
The Negro respondents [Aaron and others] appealed to
the Court of Appeals for the Eighth Circuit and also
sought there a stay [an order stopping an act] of the District Court's judgment. At the same time they . . . [asked]
us to review the District Court's judgment. . . . That we
declined to do. The Court of Appeals . . . on August 18,
1958, after convening in special session on August 4 and
hearing the appeal, reversed the District Court. On August 21, 1958, the Court of Appeals . . . permit[ted] the
School Board to petition this Court [to hear the case]. . . .
[Aaron and the others], on August 23, 1958, applied to
Justice Whittaker, as Circuit Justice for the Eighth Cir-

cuit, . . . [who] referred them to the entire Court. Recognizing the vital importance of a decision of the issues in time to permit arrangements to be made for the 1958-1959 school year, we convened in Special Term on August 28, 1958. . . . On September 12, 1958, . . . we unanimously affirmed the judgment of the Court of Appeals. . . .

In affirming the judgment of the Court of Appeals which reversed the District Court we have accepted without reservation the position of the School Board, the Superintendent of Schools, and their counsel that they displayed entire good faith in the conduct of these proceedings and in dealing with the unfortunate and distressing sequence of events which has been outlined. We likewise have accepted the findings of the District Court as to the conditions at Central High School during the 1957-1958 school year, and also the findings that the educational progress of all the students, white and colored, of that school has suffered and will continue to suffer if the conditions which prevailed last year are permitted to continue.

The significance of these findings, however, is to be considered in light of the fact, indisputably revealed by the record before us, that the conditions they depict are directly traceable to the actions of legislators and executive officials of the State of Arkansas, taken in their official capacities, which reflect their own determination to resist this Court's decision in the *Brown* case and which have brought about violent resistance to that decision in Arkansas. In its petition [to] this Court, the School Board itself describes the situation in this language: "The legislative, executive, and judicial departments of the state government opposed the desegregation of Little Rock schools by enacting laws, calling out troops, making statements villifying federal law and federal courts, and failing to utilize state law enforcement agencies and judicial processes to maintain public peace."

One may well sympathize with the position of the Board in the face of the frustrating conditions which have confronted it, but, regardless of the Board's good faith, the actions of the other state agencies responsible for those conditions compel us to reject the Board's legal position. Had Central High School been under the direct management of the State itself, it could hardly be suggested that those immediately in charge of the school should be heard to assert their own good faith as a legal excuse for delay in implementing the constitutional rights of [Aaron and the others], when vindication of those rights was rendered difficult or impossible by the actions of other state officials. The situation here is in no different posture because the members of the School Board and the Superintendent of Schools are local officials; from the point of view of the Fourteenth Amendment, they stand in this litigation as the agents of the State.

The constitutional rights of [Aaron] are not to be sacrificed or yielded to the violence and disorder which have followed upon the actions of the Governor and Legislature. As this Court said some 41 years ago in a unanimous opinion in a case involving another aspect of racial segregation [*Buchanan v. Warley*]: "It is urged that this proposed segregation will promote the public peace by preventing race conflicts. Desirable as this is, and important as is the preservation of the public peace, this aim cannot be accomplished by laws or ordinances which deny rights created or protected by the Federal Constitution." Thus law and order are not here to be preserved by depriving the Negro children of their constitutional rights.

The record before us clearly establishes that the growth of the board's difficulties to a magnitude beyond its unaided power to control is the product of state action. Those difficulties, as counsel for the Board forthrightly conceded on the oral argument in this Court, can also be brought under control by state action.

The controlling legal principles are plain. The command of the Fourteenth Amendment is that no "State" shall deny to any person within its jurisdiction the equal protection of the laws. "A State acts by its legislative, its executive, or its judicial authorities. It can act in no other way. The constitutional provision, therefore, must mean that no agency of the State, or of the officers or agents by whom its powers are exerted, shall deny to any person within its jurisdiction the equal protection of the laws. Whoever, by virtue of public position under a State government, . . . denies or takes away the equal protection of the laws, violates the constitutional inhibition; and as he acts in the name and for the State, and is clothed with the State's power, his act is that of the State. This must be so, or the constitutional prohibition has no meaning." Thus the prohibitions of the Fourteenth Amendment extend to all action of the State denying equal protection of the laws; whatever the agency of the State taking the action; or whatever the guise in which it is taken. In short, the constitutional rights of children not to be discriminated against in school admission on grounds of race or color declared by this Court in the *Brown* case can neither be nullified openly and directly by state legislators or state executive or judicial officers, nor nullified indirectly by them through evasive schemes for segregation whether attempted "ingeniously or ingenuously."

What has been said, in the light of the facts developed, is enough to dispose of the case. However, we should answer the premise of the actions of the Governor and Legislature that they are not bound by our holding in the *Brown* case. It is necessary only to recall some basic constitutional propositions which are settled doctrine.

Article VI of the Constitution makes the Constitution the "supreme Law of the Land." In 1803, Chief Justice Marshall, speaking for a unanimous Court, referring to the Constitution as "the fundamental and paramount law of the nation," declared in the notable case of *Marbury v. Madison*, that "It is emphatically the province and duty of the judicial department to say what the law is." This decision declared the basic principle that the federal judiciary is supreme in the exposition of the law of the Constitution, and that principle has ever since been respected by this Court and the Country as a permanent and indispensable feature of our constitutional system. It follows that the interpretation of the Fourteenth Amendment enunciated by this Court in the *Brown* case is the supreme law of the land, and Article VI of the Constitution makes it of binding effect on the States "any Thing in the Constitution or Laws of any State to the Contrary notwithstanding." Every state legislator and executive and judicial officer is solemnly committed by oath taken pursuant to Article VI, clause 3, "to support this Constitution." Chief Justice Taney, speaking for a unanimous Court in 1859, said that this requirement reflected the framers' "anxiety to preserve it [the Constitution] in full force, in all its powers, and to guard against resistance to or evasion of its authority, on the part of a State. . . ."

No state legislator or executive or judicial officer can war against the Constitution without violating his undertaking to support it. Chief Justice Marshall spoke for a unanimous Court in saying that: "If the legislatures of the several states may, at will, annul the judgments of the courts of the United States, and destroy the rights acquired under those judgments, the constitution itself becomes a solemn mockery. . . ." A Governor who asserts a power to nullify a federal court order is similarly restrained. If he had such power, said Chief Justice Hughes, in 1932, also for a unanimous Court, "it is manifest that the fiat of a state Governor, and not the Constitution of the United States, would be the supreme law of the land; that the restrictions of the Federal Constitution upon the exercise of state power would be but impotent phrases. . . ."

It is, of course, quite true that the responsibility for public education is primarily the concern of the States, but it is equally true that such responsibilities, like all other state activity, must be exercised consistently with federal constitutional requirements as they apply to state action. The Constitution created a government dedicated to equal justice under law. The Fourteenth Amendment embodied and emphasized that ideal. State support of segregated schools through any arrangement, management, funds, or property cannot be squared with the Amendment's command that no State shall deny to any person within its jurisdiction the equal protection of the laws. The right of a student not to be segregated on racial grounds in schools so maintained is indeed so fundamental and pervasive that it is embraced in the concept of due process of law. The basic decision in *Brown* was unanimously reached by this Court only after the case had been . . . twice argued and the issues had been given the most serious consideration. Since the first *Brown* opinion three new Justices have come to the Court. They are at one with the Justices still on the Court who participated in that basic decision as to its correctness, and that decision is now unanimously reaffirmed. The principles now announced in that decision and the obedience of the States to them, according to the command of the Constitution, are indispensable for the protection of the freedoms guaranteed by our fundamental charter for all of us. Our constitutional ideal of equal justice under law is thus made a living truth.

COURT-ORDERED BUSING

Swann v. Board of Education

[The Finger Plan] . . . desegregates all the rest of the elementary schools by the technique of grouping two or three outlying schools with one black inner city school; by transporting black students from grades one through four to the outlying white schools; and by transporting white students from the fifth and sixth grades from the outlying white schools to the inner city black school.

The Finger Plan

In 1965, in response to a lawsuit brought by the Reverend and Mrs. Darius Swann on behalf of their children, James and Edith, the Charlotte-Mecklenburg Board of Education, serving the city of Charlotte, North Carolina and the surrounding Mecklenburg County, was ordered by a Federal Court to desegregate. The Board initiated a desegregation plan based strictly on neighborhood attendance. In 1969 the Court found that the Charlotte-Mecklenburg school system, which then served 84,000 students in 107 schools, continued to be segregated. 29% percent of the school population, approximately 24,000 students, were Negroes, of whom 21,000 attended schools within the city of Charlotte. Two-thirds of those 21,000, approximately 14,000, attended just 21 segregated schools. The Federal Court ordered the Board to come up with a desegregation plan that: "[P]romises to work *now*. . . ." When the Board's Plan was found unacceptable, the plan of a Court-appointed expert, Dr. John Finger, was adopted. The Finger Plan paired inner city and suburban schools and called for the busing of students between them to achieve desegregation. The Charlotte-Mecklenburg Board of Education appealed to the United States Supreme Court.

On April 20, 1971 Chief Justice Warren Burger announced the Court's 9-0 decision. The edited text follows.

THE SWANN COURT

Chief Justice Warren Burger
Appointed by President Nixon
Served 1969 - 1986

Associate Justice Hugo Black
Appointed by President Franklin Roosevelt
Served 1937 - 1971

Associate Justice William O. Douglas
Appointed by President Franklin Roosevelt
Served 1939 - 1975

Associate Justice John M. Harlan
Appointed by President Eisenhower
Served 1955 - 1971

Associate Justice William Brennan
Appointed by President Eisenhower
Served 1956 - 1990

Associate Justice Potter Stewart
Appointed by President Eisenhower
Served 1958 - 1981

Associate Justice Byron White
Appointed by President Kennedy
Served 1962 - 1993

Associate Justice Thurgood Marshall
Appointed by President Lyndon Johnson
Served 1967 - 1991

Associate Justice Harry Blackmun
Appointed by President Nixon
Served 1970 -

The unedited text of *Swann v. Board of Education* is found on page 1, volume 402 of *United States Reports.*

SWANN v. BOARD OF EDUCATION
April 20, 1971

CHIEF JUSTICE BURGER: We granted certiorari in [agreed to hear] this case to review important issues as to the duties of school authorities and the scope of powers of federal courts under this Court's mandates to eliminate racially separate public schools established and maintained by state action.

This case and those argued with it arose in States having a long history of maintaining two sets of schools in a single school system deliberately operated to carry out a governmental policy to separate pupils in schools solely on the basis of race. That was what *Brown v. Board of Education* was all about. These cases present us with the problem of defining in more precise terms than heretofore the scope of the duty of school authorities and district courts in implementing *Brown I* and the mandate to eliminate dual systems and establish unitary systems at once. Meanwhile district courts and courts of appeals have struggled in hundreds of cases with a multitude and variety of problems under this Court's general directive. Understandably, in an area of evolving remedies, those courts had to improvise and experiment without detailed or specific guidelines. This Court, in *Brown I*, appropriately dealt with the large constitutional principles; other federal courts had to grapple with the flinty, intractable realities of day-to-day implementation of those constitutional commands. Their efforts, of necessity, embraced a process of "trial and error," and our effort to formulate guidelines must take into account their experience.

The Charlotte-Mecklenburg school system, the 43d largest in the Nation, encompasses the city of Charlotte and surrounding Mecklenburg County, North Carolina. The area is large - 550 square miles - spanning roughly 22 miles east-west and 36 miles north-south. During the 1968-1969 school year the system served more than 84,000 pupils in 107 schools. Approximately 71% of the pupils were found to be white and 29% Negro. As of June 1969 there were approximately 24,000 Negro students in the system, of whom 21,000 attended schools within the city of Charlotte. Two-thirds of those 21,000 - approximately 14,000 Negro students - attended 21 schools which were either totally Negro or more than 99% Negro.

This situation came about under a desegregation plan approved by the District Court at the commencement of the present litigation in 1965, based upon geographic zoning with a free-transfer provision. The present proceedings were initiated in September 1968 by petitioner Swann's motion for further relief based on *Green v. County School Board.* . . . All parties now agree that in 1969 the system fell short of achieving the unitary school system [required].

The District Court held numerous hearings and received voluminous evidence. In addition to finding certain actions of the school board to be discriminatory, the court also found that residential patterns in the city and county resulted in part from federal, state, and local government action other than school board decisions. School board action based on these patterns, for example, by locating schools in Negro residential areas and fixing the size of the schools to accommodate the needs of immediate neighborhoods, resulted in segregated education. These findings were subsequently accepted by the Court of Appeals.

In April 1969 the District Court ordered the school board
to come forward with a plan for both faculty and student
desegregation. Proposed plans were accepted by the court
in June and August 1969 on an interim basis only, and the
board was ordered to file a third plan by November 1969.
In November the board moved for an extension of time
until February 1970, but when that was denied the board
submitted a partially completed plan. In December 1969
the District Court held that the board's submission was
unacceptable and appointed an expert in education administration, Dr. John Finger, to prepare a desegregation plan.
Thereafter in February 1970, the District Court was presented with two alternative pupil assignment plans - the
finalized "board plan" and the "Finger plan."

The Board Plan. As finally submitted, the school board
plan closed seven schools and reassigned their pupils. It
restructured school attendance zones to achieve greater racial balance but maintained existing grade structures and
rejected techniques such as pairing and clustering as part
of a desegregation effort. The plan created a single ath-
letic league, eliminated the previously racial basis of the
school bus system, provided racially mixed faculties and
administrative staffs, and modified its free-transfer plan
into an optional majority-to-minority transfer system.

The board plan proposed substantial assignment of Negroes to nine of the system's 10 high schools, producing
17% to 36% Negro population in each. The projected Negro attendance at the 10th school, Independence, was 2%.
The proposed attendance zones for the high schools were
typically shaped like wedges of a pie, extending outward
from the center of the city to the suburban and rural
areas of the county in order to afford residents of the
center city area access to outlying schools.

As for junior high schools, the board plan rezoned the 21 school areas so that in 20 the Negro attendance would range from 0% to 38%. The other school, located in the heart of the Negro residential area, was left with an enrollment of 90% Negro.

The board plan with respect to elementary schools relied entirely upon gerrymandering of geographic zones. More than half of the Negro elementary pupils were left in nine schools that were 86% to 100% Negro; approximately half of the white elementary pupils were assigned to schools 86% to 100% white.

The Finger Plan. The plan submitted by the court-appointed expert, Dr. Finger, adopted the school board zoning plan for senior high schools with one modification: it required that an additional 300 Negro students be transported from the Negro residential area of the city to the nearly all-white Independence High School.

The Finger plan for the junior high schools employed much of the rezoning plan of the board, combined with the creation of nine "satellite" zones. Under the satellite plan, inner-city Negro students were assigned by attendance zones to nine outlying predominately white junior high schools, thereby substantially desegregating every junior high school in the system.

The Finger plan departed from the board plan chiefly in its handling of the system's 76 elementary schools. Rather than relying solely upon geographic zoning, Dr. Finger proposed use of zoning, pairing, and grouping techniques, with the result that student bodies throughout the system would range from 9% to 38% Negro.

The District Court described the plan thus:

"Like the board plan, the Finger plan does as
much by rezoning school attendance lines as can
reasonably be accomplished. However, unlike the
board plan, it does not stop there. It goes further
and desegregates all the rest of the elementary
schools by the technique of grouping two or
three outlying schools with one black inner city
school; by transporting black students from
grades one through four to the outlying white
schools; and by transporting white students from
the fifth and sixth grades from the outlying
white schools to the inner city black school."

Under the Finger plan, nine inner-city Negro schools were
grouped in this manner with 24 suburban white schools.

On February 5, 1970, the District Court adopted the
board plan, as modified by Dr. Finger, for the junior and
senior high schools. The court rejected the board elementary school plan and adopted the Finger plan as presented.
Implementation was partially stayed [stopped] by the
Court of Appeals for the Fourth Circuit on March 5, and
this Court declined to disturb the Fourth Circuit's order.

On appeal the Court of appeals affirmed [upheld] the District Court's order as to faculty desegregation and the sec-
ondary school plans, but vacated [cancelled] the order respecting elementary schools. While agreeing that the District Court properly disapproved the board plan concerning these schools, the Court of Appeals feared that the
pairing and grouping of elementary schools would place
an unreasonable burden on the board and the system's pupils. The case was remanded [sent back] to the District

Court for reconsideration and submission of further plans. This Court [agreed to hear the case] and directed reinstatement of the District Court's order pending further proceedings in that court.

On remand the District Court received two new plans for the elementary schools: a plan prepared by the United States Department of Health, Education, and Welfare (the HEW plan) based on contiguous grouping and zoning of schools, and a plan prepared by four members of the nine-member school board (the minority plan) achieving substantially the same results as the Finger plan but apparently with slightly less transportation. A majority of the school board declined to amend its proposal. After a lengthy evidentiary hearing the District Court concluded that its own plan (the Finger plan), the minority plan, and an earlier draft of the Finger plan were all reasonable and acceptable. It directed the board to adopt one of the three or in the alternative to come forward with a new, equally effective plan of its own; the court ordered that the Finger plan would remain in effect in the event the school board declined to adopt a new plan. On August 7, the board indicated it would "acquiesce" in the Finger plan, reiterating its view that the plan was unreasonable. The District Court, by order dated August 7, 1970, directed that the Finger plan remain in effect.

Nearly 17 years ago this Court held, in explicit terms, that state-imposed segregation by race in public schools denies equal protection of the laws. At no time has the Court deviated in the slightest degree from that holding or its constitutional underpinnings. None of the parties before us challenges the Court's decision of May 17, 1954, that

"in the field of public education the doctrine of
'separate but equal' has no place. Separate educational facilities are inherently unequal. Therefore, we hold that the plaintiffs and others similarly situated . . . are, by reason of the segregation
complained of, deprived of the equal protection
of the laws guaranteed by the Fourteenth
Amendment. . . .

"Because these are class actions [cases brought by
a group of people with similar characteristics],
because of the wide applicability of this decision,
and because of the great variety of local conditions, the formulation of decrees in these cases
presents problems of considerable complexity."

None of the parties before us questions the Court's 1955
holding in *Brown II,* that

"School authorities have the primary responsibility for elucidating, assessing, and solving these
problems; courts will have to consider whether
the action of school authorities constitutes good
faith implementation of the governing constitutional principles. Because of their proximity to
local conditions and the possible need for further
hearings, the courts which originally heard these
cases can best perform this judicial appraisal.
Accordingly, we believe it appropriate to remand
the cases to those courts.

"In fashioning and effectuating the decrees, the
courts will be guided by equitable principles.
Traditionally, equity [fairness] has been characterized by a practical flexibility in shaping its

remedies and by a facility for adjusting and reconciling public and private needs. These cases
call for the exercise of these traditional attributes
of equity power. At stake is the personal interest
of the plaintiffs in admission to public schools as
soon as practicable on a nondiscriminatory basis.
To effectuate this interest may call for elimination of a variety of obstacles in making the transition to school systems operated in accordance
with the constitutional principles set forth in our
May 17, 1954, decision. Courts of equity may
properly take into account the public interest in
the elimination of such obstacles in a systematic
and effective manner. But it should go without
saying that the vitality of these constitutional
principles cannot be allowed to yield simply because of disagreement with them."

Over the 16 years since *Brown II,* many difficulties were
encountered in implementation of the basic constitutional
requirement that the State not discriminate between public school children on the basis of their race. Nothing in
our national experience prior to 1955 prepared anyone
for dealing with changes and adjustments of the magnitude and complexity encountered since then. Deliberate
resistance of some to the Court's mandates has impeded
the good-faith efforts of others to bring school systems
into compliance. The detail and nature of these dilatory
tactics have been noted frequently by this Court and other
courts.

By the time the Court considered *Green v. County School
Board,* in 1968, very little progress had been made in
many areas where dual school systems had historically
been maintained by operation of state laws. In *Green,* the

Court was confronted with a record of a freedom-of-choice program that the District Court had found to operate in fact to preserve a dual system more than a decade after *Brown II.* While acknowledging that a freedom-of-choice concept could be a valid remedial measure in some circumstances, its failure to be effective in *Green* required that:

"The burden on a school board today is to come forward with a plan that promises realistically to work . . . *now* . . . until it is clear that state-imposed segregation has been completely removed."

This was plain language, yet the 1969 Term of Court brought fresh evidence of the dilatory tactics of many school authorities. *Alexander v. Holmes County Board of Education* restated the basic obligation asserted in *Griffin v. School Board* and *Green,* that the remedy must be implemented *forthwith.*

The problems encountered by the district courts and courts of appeals make plain that we should now try to amplify guidelines, however incomplete and imperfect, for the assistance of school authorities and courts. The failure of local authorities to meet their constitutional obligations aggravated the massive problem of converting from the state-enforced discrimination of racially separate school systems. This process has been rendered more difficult by changes since 1954 in the structure and patterns of communities, the growth of student population, movement of families, and other changes, some of which had marked impact on school planning, sometimes neutralizing or negating remedial action before it was fully implemented. Rural areas accustomed for half a century to the consolidated school systems implemented by bus transportation could make adjustments more readily than metropolitan areas with dense and shifting population, numerous schools, congested and complex traffic patterns.

The objective today remains to eliminate from the public schools all vestiges of state-imposed segregation. Segregation was the evil struck down by *Brown I* as contrary to the equal protection guarantees of the Constitution. That was the violation sought to be corrected by the remedial measures of *Brown II*. That was the basis for the holding in *Green* that school authorities are "clearly charged with the affirmative duty to take whatever steps might be necessary to convert to a unitary system in which racial discrimination would be eliminated root and branch."

If school authorities fail in their affirmative obligations under these holdings, judicial authority may be invoked. Once a right and a violation have been shown, the scope of a district court's equitable powers to remedy past wrongs is broad, for breadth and flexibility are inherent in equitable remedies.

. . . . This allocation of responsibility once made, the Court attempted from time to time to provide some guidelines for the exercise of the district judge's discretion and for the reviewing function of the courts of appeals. However, a school desegregation case does not differ fundamentally from other cases involving the framing of equitable remedies to repair the denial of a constitutional right. The task is to correct, by a balancing of the individual and collective interests, the condition that offends the Constitution.

In seeking to define even in broad and general terms how far this remedial power extends it is important to remember that judicial powers may be exercised only on the basis of a constitutional violation. Remedial judicial authority does not put judges automatically in the shoes of school authorities whose powers are plenary [broad]. Judicial authority enters only when local authority defaults.

School authorities are traditionally charged with broad power to formulate and implement educational policy and might well conclude, for example, that in order to prepare students to live in a pluralistic society each school should have a prescribed ratio of Negro to white students reflecting the proportion for the district as a whole. To do this as an educational policy is within the broad discretionary powers of school authorities; absent a finding of a constitutional violation, however, that would not be within the authority of a federal court. As with any equity case, the nature of the violation determines the scope of the remedy. In default by the school authorities of their obligation to proffer acceptable remedies, a district court has broad power to fashion a remedy that will assure a unitary school system.

The school authorities argue that the equity powers of federal district courts have been limited by Title IV of the Civil Rights Act of 1964. The language and the history of Title IV show that it was enacted not to limit but to define the role of the Federal Government in the implementation of the *Brown I* decision. It authorizes the Commissioner of Education to provide technical assistance to local boards in the preparation of desegregation plans, to arrange "training institutes" for school personnel involved in desegregation efforts, and to make grants directly to schools to ease the transition to unitary systems. It also authorizes the Attorney General, in specified circumstances, to initiate federal desegregation suits. Section 2000c(b) defines "desegregation" as it is used in Title IV:

> "'Desegregation' means the assignment of students to public schools and within such schools without regard to their race, color, religion, or national origin, but 'desegregation' shall not mean the assignment of students to public schools in order to overcome racial imbalance."

Section 2000c-6, authorizing the Attorney General to institute federal suits, contains the following proviso:

> "nothing herein shall empower any official or court of the United States to issue any order seeking to achieve a racial balance in any school by requiring the transportation of pupils or students from one school to another or one school district to another in order to achieve such racial balance, or otherwise enlarge the existing power of the court to insure compliance with constitutional standards."

On their face, the sections quoted purport only to insure that the provisions of Title IV of the Civil Rights Act of 1964 will not be read as granting new powers. The proviso in Section 2000c-6 is in terms designed to foreclose any interpretation of the Act as expanding the *existing* powers of federal courts to enforce the Equal Protection Clause. There is no suggestion of an intention to restrict those powers or withdraw from courts their historic equitable remedial powers. The legislative history of Title IV indicates that Congress was concerned that the Act might be read as creating a right of action under the Fourteenth

Amendment in the situation of so-called "de facto segregation," where racial imbalance exists in the schools but with no showing that this was brought about by discriminatory action of state authorities. In short, there is nothing in the Act that provides us material assistance in answering the question of remedy for state-imposed segregation in violation of *Brown I*. The basis of our decision must be the prohibition of the Fourteenth Amendment that no State shall "deny to any person within its jurisdiction the equal protection of the laws."

We turn now to the problem of defining with more particularity the responsibilities of school authorities in desegregating a state-enforced dual school system in light of the Equal Protection Clause....

In *Green*, we pointed out that existing policy and practice with regard to faculty, staff, transportation, extracurricular activities, and facilities were among the most important indicia of a segregated system. Independent of student assignment, where it is possible to identify a "white school" or a "Negro school" simply by reference to the racial composition of teachers and staff, the quality of school buildings and equipment, or the organization of sports activities, a *prima facie* [on the face of it] case of violation of substantive constitutional rights under the Equal Protection Clause is shown.

When a system has been dual in these respects, the first remedial responsibility of school authorities is to eliminate invidious racial distinctions. With respect to such matters as transportation, supporting personnel, and extracurricular activities, no more than this may be necessary. Similar corrective action must be taken with regard to the maintenance of buildings and the distribution of equipment. In these areas, normal administrative practice should produce schools of like quality, facilities, and staffs. Something more must be said, however, as to faculty assignment and new school construction.

. . . . In *United States v. Montgomery County Board of Education*, the District Court set as a goal a plan of faculty assignment in each school with a ratio of white to Negro faculty members substantially the same throughout the system. This order was predicated on the District Court finding that:

> "The evidence does not reflect any real administrative problems involved in immediately desegregating the substitute teachers, the student teachers, the night school faculties, and in the evolvement of a really legally adequate program for the substantial desegregation of the faculties of all schools in the system commencing with the school year 1968-69."

The District Court in *Montgomery* then proceeded to set an initial ratio for the whole system of at least two Negro teachers out of each 12 in any given school. The Court of Appeals modified the order by eliminating what it regarded as "fixed mathematical" ratios of faculty and substituted an initial requirement of "*substantially* or *approximately*" a five-to-one ratio. With respect to the future, the Court of Appeals held that the numerical ratio should be eliminated and that compliance should not be tested solely by the achievement of specified proportions.

We reversed the Court of Appeals and restored the District Court's order in its entirety, holding that the order of the District Judge "was adopted in the spirit of this Court's opinion in *Green*... in that his plan 'promises realistically to work, and promises realistically to work *now*.' The modifications ordered by the panel of the Court of Appeals, while of course not intended to do so, would, we think, take from the order some of its capacity to expedite, by means of specific commands, the day when a completely unified, unitary, nondiscriminatory school system becomes a reality instead of a hope...."

The principles of *Montgomery* have been properly followed by the District Court and the Court of Appeals in this case.

The construction of new schools and the closing of old ones are two of the most important functions of local school authorities and also two of the most complex. They must decide questions of location and capacity in light of population growth, finances, land values, site availability, through an almost endless list of factors to be considered. The result of this will be a decision which, when combined with one technique or another of student assignment, will determine the racial composition of the student body in each school in the system. Over the long run, the consequences of the choices will be far reaching. People gravitate toward school facilities, just as schools are located in response to the needs of people. The location of schools may thus influence the patterns of residential development of a metropolitan area and have important impact on composition of inner-city neighborhoods.

In the past, choices in this respect have been used as a potent weapon for creating or maintaining a state-segregated school system. In addition to the classic pattern of building schools specifically intended for Negro or white students, school authorities have sometimes, since *Brown*, closed schools which appeared likely to become racially mixed through changes in neighborhood residential patterns. This was sometimes accompanied by building new schools in the areas of white suburban expansion farthest from Negro population centers in order to maintain the separation of the races with a minimum departure from the formal principles of "neighborhood zoning." Such a policy does more than simply influence the short-run composition of the student body of a new school. It may well promote segregated residential patterns which, when combined with "neighborhood zoning," further lock the school system into a mold of separation of the races. Upon a proper showing a district court may consider this in fashioning a remedy.

In ascertaining the existence of legally imposed school segregation, the existence of a pattern of school construction and abandonment is thus a factor of great weight. In devising remedies where legally imposed segregation has been established, it is the responsibility of local authorities and district courts to see to it that future school construction and abandonment are not used and do not serve to perpetuate or re-establish the dual system. When necessary, district courts should retain jurisdiction to assure that these responsibilities are carried out.

The central issue in this case is that of student assignment, and there are essentially four problem areas:

(1) to what extent racial balance or racial quotas may be used as an implement in a remedial order to correct a previously segregated system;

(2) whether every all-Negro and all-white school must be eliminated as an indispensable part of a remedial process of desegregation;

(3) what the limits are, if any, on the rearrangement of school districts and attendance zones, as a remedial measure; and

(4) what the limits are, if any, on the use of transportation facilities to correct state-enforced racial school segregation.

(1) *Racial Balances or Racial Quotas.*

The constant theme and thrust of every holding from *Brown I* to date is that state-enforced separation of races in public schools is discrimination that violates the Equal Protection Clause. The remedy commanded was to dismantle dual school systems.

We are concerned in [this case] with the elimination of the discrimination inherent in the dual school systems, not with myriad factors of human existence which can cause discrimination in a multitude of ways on racial, religious, or ethnic grounds. The target of the cases from *Brown I* to the present was the dual school system. The elimination of racial discrimination in public schools is a large task and one that should not be retarded by efforts to achieve broader purposes lying beyond the jurisdiction of school authorities. One vehicle can carry only a limited amount of baggage. It would not serve the important objective of *Brown I* to seek to use school desegregation cases for purposes beyond their scope, although desegregation of schools ultimately will have impact on other forms of discrimination. . . .

Our objective in dealing with the issues presented by [this case] is to see that school authorities exclude no pupil of a racial minority from any school, directly or indirectly, on account of race; it does not and cannot embrace all the problems of racial prejudice, even when those problems contribute to disproportionate racial concentrations in some schools.

In this case it is urged that the District Court has imposed a racial balance requirement of 71%-29% on individual schools. The fact that no such objective was actually achieved - and would appear to be impossible - tends to blunt that claim, yet in the opinion and order of the District Court of December 1, 1969, we find that court directing

> "that efforts should be made to reach a 71-29 ratio in the various schools so that there will be no basis for contending that one school is racially different from the others . . . , [t]hat no school [should] be operated with an all-black or predominantly black student body, [and] [t]hat pupils of all grades [should] be assigned in such a way that as nearly as practicable the various schools at various grade levels have about the same proportion of black and white students."

The District Judge went on to acknowledge that variation "from that norm may be unavoidable." This contains intimations that the "norm" is a fixed mathematical racial balance reflecting the pupil constituency of the system. If we were to read the holding of the District Court to require . . . any particular degree of racial balance or mixing, that approach would be disapproved and we would be obliged to reverse. The constitutional command to desegregate schools does not mean that every school in every community must always reflect the racial composition of the school system as a whole.

As the voluminous record in this case shows, the predicate for the District Court's use of the 71%-29% ratio was twofold: first, its express finding . . . that a dual school system had been maintained by the school authorities at least until 1969; second, its finding . . . that the school board had totally defaulted in its acknowledged duty to come forward with an acceptable plan of its own, notwithstanding the patient efforts of the District Judge who, on at least three occasions, urged the board to submit plans. . . . It was because of this total failure of the school board that the District Court was obliged to turn to other qualified sources, and Dr. Finger was designated to assist the District Court to do what the board should have done.

We see therefore that the use made of mathematical ratios was no more than a starting point in the process of shaping a remedy, rather than an inflexible requirement. From that starting point the District Court proceeded to frame a decree that was within its discretionary powers, as an equitable remedy for the particular circumstances. As we said in *Green*, a school authority's remedial plan or a district court's remedial decree is to be judged by its effectiveness. Awareness of the racial composition of the whole school system is likely to be a useful starting point in shaping a remedy to correct past constitutional violations. In sum, the very limited use made of mathematical ratios was within the equitable remedial discretion of the District Court.

(2) *One-race Schools.*

The record in this case reveals the familiar phenomenon that in metropolitan areas minority groups are often found concentrated in one part of the city. In some circumstances certain schools may remain all or largely of one race until new schools can be provided or neighborhood patterns change. Schools all or predominately of one race in a district of mixed population will require close scrutiny to determine that school assignments are not part of state-enforced segregation.

In light of the above, it should be clear that the existence of some small number of one-race, or virtually one-race, schools within a district is not in and of itself the mark of a system that still practices segregation by law. The district judge or school authorities should make every effort to achieve the greatest possible degree of actual desegregation and will thus necessarily be concerned with the elimination of one-race schools. No *per se* [inherent] rule can adequately embrace all the difficulties of reconciling the competing interests involved; but in a system with a history of segregation the need for remedial criteria of sufficient specificity to assure a school authority's compliance with its constitutional duty warrants a presumption against schools that are substantially disproportionate in their racial composition. Where the school authority's proposed plan for conversion from a dual to a unitary system contemplates the continued existence of some schools that are all or predominately of one race, they have the burden of showing that such school assignments are genuinely nondiscriminatory. The court should scrutinize such schools, and the burden upon the school authorities will be to satisfy the court that their racial composition is not the result of present or past discriminatory action on their part.

An optional majority-to-minority transfer provision has long been recognized as a useful part of every desegregation plan. Provision for optional transfer of those in the majority racial group of a particular school to other schools where they will be in the minority is an indispensable remedy for those students willing to transfer to other schools in order to lessen the impact on them of the state-imposed stigma of segregation. In order to be effective, such a transfer arrangement must grant the transferring student free transportation and space must be made available in the school to which he desires to move. The court orders in this . . . case now provide such an option.

(3) *Remedial Altering of Attendance Zones.*

The maps submitted in these cases graphically demonstrate that one of the principal tools employed by school planners and by courts to break up the dual school system has been a frank - and sometimes drastic - gerrymandering of school districts and attendance zones. An additional step was pairing, "clustering," or "grouping" of schools with attendance assignments made deliberately to accomplish the transfer of Negro students out of formerly segregated Negro schools and transfer of white students to formerly all-negro schools. More often than not, these zones are neither compact nor contiguous; indeed they may be on opposite ends of the city. As an interim corrective measure, this cannot be said to be beyond the broad remedial powers of a court.

Absent a constitutional violation there would be no basis for judicially ordering assignment of students on a racial basis. All things being equal, with no history of discrimination, it might well be desirable to assign pupils to schools nearest their homes. But all things are not equal in a system that has been deliberately constructed and maintained to enforce racial segregation. The remedy for such segregation may be administratively awkward, inconvenient, and even bizarre in some situations and may impose burdens on some; but all awkwardness and inconvenience cannot be avoided in the interim period when remedial adjustments are being made to eliminate the dual school systems.

No fixed or even substantially fixed guidelines can be established as to how far a court can go, but it must be recognized that there are limits. The objective is to dismantle the dual school system. "Racially neutral" assignment plans proposed by school authorities to a district court may be inadequate; such plans may fail to counteract the continuing effects of past school segregation resulting from discriminatory location of school sites or distortion of school size in order to achieve or maintain an artificial racial separation. When school authorities present a district court with a "loaded game board," affirmative action in the form of remedial altering of attendance zones is proper to achieve truly non-discriminatory assignments. In short, an assignment plan is not acceptable simply because it appears to be neutral.

In this area, we must of necessity rely to a large extent, as this Court has for more than 16 years, on the informed judgment of the district courts in the first instance and on courts of appeals.

We hold that the pairing and grouping of noncontiguous school zones is a permissible tool and such action is to be considered in light of the objectives sought. Judicial steps in shaping such zones going beyond combinations of contiguous areas should be examined in light of what is said in subdivisions (1), (2), and (3) of this opinion concerning the objectives to be sought. Maps do not tell the whole story since noncontiguous school zones may be more accessible to each other in terms of the critical travel time, because of traffic patterns and good highways, than schools geographically closer together. Conditions in different localities will vary so widely that no rigid rules can be laid down to govern all situations.

(4) *Transportation of Students.*

The scope of permissible transportation of students as an implement of a remedial decree has never been defined by this Court and by the very nature of the problem it cannot be defined with precision. No rigid guidelines as to student transportation can be given for application to the infinite variety of problems presented in thousands of situations. Bus transportations has been an integral part of the public education system for years, and was perhaps the single most important factor in the transition from the one-room schoolhouse to the consolidated school. Eighteen million of the Nation's public school children, approximately 39%, were transported to their schools by bus in 1969-1970 in all parts of the country.

The importance of bus transportation as a normal and accepted tool of educational policy is readily discernible in this . . . case. The Charlotte school authorities did not purport to assign students on the basis of geographically drawn zones until 1965 and then they allowed almost unlimited transfer privileges. The District Court's conclusion that assignment of children to the school nearest their home serving their grade would not produce an effective dismantling of the dual system is supported by the record.

Thus the remedial techniques used in the District Court's order were within that court's power to provide equitable relief; implementation of the decree is well within the capacity of the school authority.

The decree provided that the buses used to implement the plan would operate on direct routes. Students would be picked up at schools near their homes and transported to the schools they were to attend. The trips for elementary school pupils average about seven miles and the District Court found that they would take "not over 35 minutes at the most." This system compares favorably with the transportation plan previously operated in Charlotte under which each day 23,600 students on all grade levels were transported an average of 15 miles one way for an average trip requiring over an hour. In these circumstances, we find no basis for holding that the local school authorities may not be required to employ bus transportation as one tool of school desegregation. Desegregation plans cannot be limited to the walk-in school.

An objection to transportation of students may have validity when the time or distance of travel is so great as to either risk the health of the children or significantly impinge on the educational process. District courts must weigh the soundness of any transportation plan in light of what is said in subdivisions (1), (2), and (3) above. It hardly needs stating that the limits on time of travel will vary with many factors, but probably with none more than the age of the students. The reconciliation of competing values in a desegregation case is, of course, a difficult task with many sensitive facets but fundamentally no more so than remedial measures courts of equity have traditionally employed.

The Court of Appeals, searching for a term to define the equitable remedial power of the district courts, used the term "reasonableness." In *Green*, this Court used the term "feasible" and by implication, "workable," "effective," and "realistic" in the mandate to develop "a plan that promises realistically to work, and . . . to work *now.*" On the facts of this case, we are unable to conclude that the order of the District Court is not reasonable, feasible and workable. However, in seeking to define the scope of remedial power or the limits on remedial power of courts in an area as sensitive as we deal with here, words are poor instruments to convey the sense of basic fairness inherent in equity. Substance, not semantics, must govern, and we have sought to suggest the nature of limitations without frustrating the appropriate scope of equity.

At some point, these school authorities and others like them should have achieved full compliance with this Court's decision in *Brown I.* The systems would then be "unitary" in the sense required by our decisions in *Green* and *Alexander.*

It does not follow that the communities served by such systems will remain demographically stable, for in a growing, mobile society, few will do so. Neither school authorities nor district courts are constitutionally required to make year-by-year adjustments of the racial composition of student bodies once the affirmative duty to desegregate has been accomplished and racial discrimination through official action is eliminated from the system. This does not mean that federal courts are without power to deal

with future problems; but in the absence of a showing
that either the school authorities or some other agency of
the State has deliberately attempted to fix or alter demographic patterns to affect the racial composition of the
schools, further intervention by a district court should not
be necessary.

For the reasons herein set forth, the judgment of the
Court of Appeals is affirmed as to those parts in which it
affirmed the judgment of the District Court. The order
of the District Court, dated August 7, 1970, is also affirmed. It is so ordered.

THE RIGHT TO VOTE

Nixon v. Herndon

[I]n no event shall a negro be eligible to participate in a democratic party primary election.
The Texas Democratic Primary Statute

The Fifteenth Amendment says that the right of citizens to vote cannot not be denied by the States on account of race or color. In 1923 Texas, a one-party state, asserting that a primary election was not covered by the Fifteenth Amendment, forbade negroes the right to vote in primaries. Dr. L.A. Nixon, a negro, was denied the right to vote in the 1924 Texas Democratic Primary held in El Paso, Texas, solely on account of his race. Dr. Nixon sued the Judges of Election for damages, asserting a violation of the Fourteenth and Fifteenth Amendments. On March 7, 1927 Justice Oliver Wendell Holmes, Jr. announced the Court's 9-0 decision. The edited text follows.

Nixon v. Condon

[A]ll white democrats who are qualified . . . and none other be allowed to participate in the primary elections.
The Texas Democratic Party Resolution

To evade the Court's decision in *Nixon v. Herndon,* Texas enacted a new law giving every political party in the state the power to determine who was qualified to vote in their primary elections. The Executive Committee of the Texas Democratic Party, acting under this statute, adopted a resolution that only white democrats could vote in their primaries. In the 1928 Texas Democratic Primary, Nixon was again denied the right to vote based solely on his race. Dr. Nixon again sued the Judges of Election for damages, asserting a further violation of his Fourteenth and Fifteenth Amendment rights. On March 15, 1932 Justice Benjamin Cardozo announced the 5-4 decision of the Court. The edited text follows.

THE NIXON I COURT

Chief Justice William Howard Taft
Appointed by President Harding
Served 1921 - 1930

Associate Justice Oliver Wendell Holmes, Jr.
Appointed by President Theodore Roosevelt
Served 1902 - 1932

Associate Justice Willis Van Devanter
Appointed by President Taft
Served 1910 - 1937

Associate Justice James McReynolds
Appointed by President Wilson
Served 1914 - 1941

Associate Justice Louis Brandeis
Appointed by President Wilson
Served 1916 - 1939

Associate Justice George Sutherland
Appointed by President Harding
Served 1922 - 1938

Associate Justice Pierce Butler
Appointed by President Harding
Served 1922 - 1939

Associate Justice Edward Sanford
Appointed by President Harding
Served 1923 - 1930

Associate Justice Harlan Fiske Stone
Appointed by President Coolidge
Served 1925 - 1946

The unedited text of *Nixon v. Herndon* can be found on
page 536, volume 273 of *United States Reports.*

NIXON v. HERNDON
March 7, 1927

JUSTICE HOLMES: This is an action against the Judges of Elections [represented here by Herndon] for refusing to permit the plaintiff [Nixon] to vote at a primary election in Texas. It lays the damages at five thousand dollars. The petition alleges that [Nixon] is a negro, a citizen of the United States and of Texas and a resident of El Paso, and in every way qualified to vote, as set forth in detail, except that the statute to be mentioned interferes with his right; that on July 26, 1924, a primary election was held at El Paso for the nomination of candidates for a senator and representatives in Congress and State and other offices, upon the Democratic ticket; that [Nixon], being a member of the Democratic party, sought to vote but was denied the right, by [Herndon]; that the denial was based upon a Statute of Texas enacted in May, 1923, and designated Article 3093a, by the words of which "in no event shall a negro be eligible to participate in a Democratic party primary election held in the State of Texas," etc., and that this statute is contrary to the Fourteenth and Fifteenth Amendments to the Constitution of the United States. [Herndon] moved to dismiss upon the ground that the subject matter of the suit was political and not within the jurisdiction of the Court and that no violation of the Amendments was shown. The suit was dismissed and [appealed] directly to this Court. Here no argument was made on behalf of [Herndon] but a brief [a written statement of the case] was allowed to be filed by the Attorney General of the State.

The objection that the subject matter of the suit is political is little more than a play upon words. Of course the petition concerns political action but it alleges and seeks to recover for private damage. That private damage may be caused by such political action and may be recovered for in a suit at law hardly has been doubted for over two hundred years, since *Ashby v. White*, and has been recognized by this Court. If [Herndon's] conduct was a wrong to [Nixon] the same reasons that allow a recovery for denying [Nixon] a vote at a final election allow it for denying a vote at the primary election that may determine the final result.

The important question is whether the statute can be sustained [maintained]. But although we state it as a question the answer does not seem to us open to a doubt. We find it unnecessary to consider the Fifteenth Amendment, because it seems to us hard to imagine a more direct and obvious infringement of the Fourteenth. That Amendment, while it applies to all, was passed, as we know, with a special intent to protect the blacks from discrimination against them. That Amendment "not only gave citizenship and the privileges of citizenship to persons of color, but it denied to any State the power to withhold from them the equal protection of the laws. . . . What is this but declaring that the law in the States shall be the same for the black as for the white; that all persons, whether colored or white, shall stand equal before the laws of the States, and, in regard to the colored race, for whose protection the amendment was primarily designed, that no discrimination shall be made against them by law because of their color?" The statute of Texas in the teeth of the prohibitions referred to assumes to forbid negroes to take part in a primary election the importance of which we have indicated, discriminating against them by the distinction of color alone. States may do a good deal of classifying that it is difficult to believe rational, but there are limits, and it is too clear for extended argument that color cannot be made the basis of a statutory classification affecting the right set up in this case.

Judgment reversed.

THE NIXON II COURT

Chief Justice Charles Evans Hughes
Appointed by President Hoover
Served 1930 - 1941

Associate Justice Oliver Wendell Holmes, Jr.
Appointed by President Theodore Roosevelt
Served 1902 - 1932

Associate Justice Willis Van Devanter
Appointed by President Taft
Served 1910 - 1937

Associate Justice James McReynolds
Appointed by President Wilson
Served 1914 - 1941

Associate Justice Louis Brandeis
Appointed by President Wilson
Served 1916 - 1939

Associate Justice George Sutherland
Appointed by President Harding
Served 1922 - 1938

Associate Justice Pierce Butler
Appointed by President Harding
Served 1922 - 1939

Associate Justice Harlan Fiske Stone
Appointed by President Coolidge
Served 1925 - 1946

Associate Justice Owen Roberts
Appointed by President Hoover
Served 1930 - 1945

The unedited text of *Nixon v. Condon* can be found on page 73, volume 286 of *United States Reports*.

NIXON v. CONDON
May 2, 1932

JUSTICE CARDOZO: The petitioner [Nixon], a Negro, has brought this action against judges of election in Texas [represented here by Condon] to recover damages for their refusal by reason of his race or color to permit him to cast his vote at a primary election.

This is not the first time that he has found it necessary to invoke the jurisdiction of the federal courts in vindication of privileges secured to him by the Federal Constitution.

In *Nixon v. Herndon*, decided at the October Term, 1926, this court had before it a statute of the State of Texas whereby the legislature had said that "in no event shall a negro be eligible to participate in a democratic party primary election [held in that State]," and that "should a negro vote in a democratic primary election, the ballot shall be void," and election officials were directed to throw it out. While the mandate was in force, the Negro was shut out from a share in primary elections, not in obedience to the will of the party speaking through the party organs, but by the command of the State itself, speaking by the voice of its chosen representatives. At the suit of [Nixon], the statute was adjudged void as an infringement of his rights and liberties under the Constitution of the United States.

Promptly after the announcement of that decision, the legislature of Texas enacted a new statute repealing the article condemned by this court; declaring that the effect of the decision was to create an emergency with a need for immediate action; and substituting for the article so repealed another bearing the same number. By the article thus substituted, "every political party in this State through its State Executive Committee shall have the power to prescribe the qualifications of its own members and shall in its own way determine who shall be qualified to vote or otherwise participate in such political party; provided that no person shall ever be denied the right to participate in a primary in this State because of former political views or affiliations or because of membership or non-membership in organizations other than the political party."

Acting under the new statute, the State Executive Committee of the Democratic party adopted a resolution "that all white democrats who are qualified under the constitution and laws of Texas and who subscribe to the statutory pledge provided in [the Election Law], and none other, be allowed to participate in the primary elections to be held July 28, 1928, and August 25, 1928," and the chairman and secretary were directed to forward copies of the resolution to the committees in the several counties.

On July 28, 1928, [Nixon], a citizen of the United States, and qualified to vote unless disqualified by the foregoing resolution, presented himself at the polls and requested that he be furnished with a ballot. [Condon] declined to furnish the ballot or to permit the vote on the ground that the petitioner was a Negro and that by force of the resolution of the Executive Committee only white Democrats were allowed to be voters at the Democratic primary. The refusal was followed by this action for damages. In the District Court there was a judgment of dismissal, which was affirmed [upheld] by the Circuit Court of Appeals for the Fifth Circuit. [Appeal] brings the cause here.

Barred from voting at a primary [Nixon] has been, and this for the sole reason that his color is not white. The result for him is no different from what it was when his cause was here before. The argument for [Condon] is, however, that identity of result has been attained through essential diversity of method. We are reminded that the Fourteenth Amendment is a restraint upon the States and not upon private persons unconnected with a State. This line of demarcation drawn, we are told that a political party is merely a voluntary association; that it has inherent power like voluntary associations generally to determine its own membership; that the new article of the statute, adopted in place of the mandatory article of exclusion condemned by this court, has no other effect than to restore to the members of the party the power that would have been theirs if the lawmakers had been silent; and that qualifications thus established are as far aloof from the impact of constitutional restraint as those for membership in a golf club or for admission to a Masonic lodge.

Whether a political party in Texas has inherent power today without restraint by any law to determine its own membership, we are not required at this time either to affirm or to deny. The argument for [Nixon] is that quite apart from the article in controversy, there are other provisions of the Election Law whereby the privilege of unfettered choice has been withdrawn or abridged; that nomination at a primary is in many circumstances required by the statute if nomination is to be made at all; that parties and their representatives have become the custodians of official power; and that if heed is to be given to the realities of political life, they are now agencies of the State, the instruments by which government becomes a living thing. In that view, so runs the argument, a party is still free to define for itself the political tenets of its members, but to those who profess its tenets there may be no denial of its privileges.

A narrower base will serve for our judgment in the cause at hand. Whether the effect of Texas legislation has been to work so complete a transformation of the concept of a political party as a voluntary association, we do not now decide. Nothing in this opinion is to be taken as carrying with it an intimation that the court is ready or unready to follow [Nixon] so far. As to that, decision must be postponed until decision becomes necessary. Whatever our conclusion might be if the statute had remitted to the party the untrammeled power to prescribe the qualifications of its members, nothing of the kind was done. Instead, the statute lodged the power in a committee, which excluded [Nixon] and others of his race, not by virtue of any authority delegated by the party, but by virtue of an authority originating or supposed to originate in the mandate of the law.

We recall at this point the wording of the statute invoked by [Condon]. "Every political party in this State through its State Executive Committee shall have the power to prescribe the qualifications of its own members and shall in its own way determine who shall be qualified to vote or otherwise participate in such political party." Whatever inherent power a State political party has to determine the content of its membership resides in the State convention. There platforms of principles are announced and the tests of party allegiance made known to the world. What is true in that regard of parties generally, is true more particularly in Texas, where the statute is explicit in committing to the State convention the formulation of the party faith. The State Executive Committee, if it is the sovereign organ of the party, is not such by virtue of any powers inherent in its being. It is, as its name imports, a committee and nothing more, a committee to be chosen by the convention and to consist of a chairman and thirty-one members, one from each senatorial district of the State. To this committee the statute here in controversy has attempted to confide authority to determine of its own motion the requisites of party membership and in so doing to speak for the party as a whole. Never has the State convention made declaration of a will to bar Negroes of the State from admission to the party ranks. Counsel for [Condon] so conceded upon the hearing in this court. Whatever power of exclusion has been exercised by the members of the committee has come to them, therefore, not as the delegates of the party, but as the delegates of the State. Indeed, adherence to the statute leads to the conclusion that a resolution once adopted by the committee must continue to be binding upon the judges of election though the party in convention may have sought to override it, unless the committee, yielding to the moral force of numbers, shall revoke its earlier action and obey the party will. Power so intrenched is statutory, not inherent. If the State had not conferred it, there would be hardly color of right to give a basis for its exercise.

. . . . The ruling in the first case was directed to the validity of the provision whereby neither the party nor the committee is to be permitted to make former political affiliations the test of party regularity. There were general observations in the opinion as to the functions of parties and committees. They do not constitute the decision. The decision was merely this, that "the committee whether viewed as an agency of the State or as a mere agency of the party is not authorized to take any action which is forbidden by an express and valid statute." The ruling in the second case, which does not come from the highest court of the State, upholds the constitutionality of [the Election Law] as amended in 1927, and speaks of the exercise of the inherent powers of the party by the act of its proper officers. There is nothing to show, however, that the mind of the court was directed to the point that the members of a committee would not have been the proper officers to exercise the inherent powers of the party if the statute had not attempted to clothe them with that quality. The management of the affairs of a group already associated together as members of a party is obviously a very different function from that of determining who the members of the group shall be. If another view were to be accepted, a committee might rule out of the party a faction distasteful to itself, and exclude the very men who had helped to bring it into existence. In any event, the Supreme Court of Texas has not yet spoken on the subject with clearness or finality, and nothing in its pronouncements brings us to the belief that in the absence of a statute or other express grant it would recognize a mere committee as invested with all the powers of the party assembled in convention. Indeed, its latest decision dealing with any aspect of the statute here in controversy, a decision handed down on April 21, 1932, describes the statute as constituting "a grant of power" to the State Executive Committee to determine who shall participate in the primary elections. What was questioned in that case was the validity of a pledge exacted from the voters that it was their *bona fide* purpose to support the party nominees. The court in upholding the exaction found a basis for its ruling in another article of the [Texas] Statutes, in an article of the Penal Code, and in the inherent power of the committee to adopt regulations reasonably designed to give effect to the obligation assumed by an elector in the very act of voting. To clinch the argument the court then added that if all these sources of authority were inadequate, the legislature had made in [the Election Law] an express "grant of power" to determine qualifications generally. There is no suggestion in the opinion that the inherent power of the committee was broad enough (apart from legislation) to permit it to prescribe the extent of party membership, to say to a group of voters, ready as was [Nixon] to take the statutory pledge, that one class should be eligible and another not. On the contrary, the whole opinion is instinct with the concession that pretensions so extraordinary must find their warrant in a statute. The most that can be said for [Condon] is that the inherent powers of the Committee are still unsettled in the local courts. Nothing in the state of the decisions requires us to hold that they have been settled in a manner that would be subversive of the fundamental postulates of party organization. The suggestion is offered that in default of inherent power or of statutory grant the committee may have been armed with the requisite authority by vote of the convention. Neither at our bar nor on the trial was the case presented on that theory. At every stage of the case the assumption has been made that authority, if there was any, was either the product of the statute or was inherent in the committee under the law of its creation.

We discover no significance, and surely no significance favorable to [Condon], in earlier acts of legislation whereby the power to prescribe additional qualifications was conferred on local committees in the several counties of the State. The very fact that such legislation was thought necessary is a token that the committees were without inherent power. We do not impugn the competence of the legislature to designate the agencies whereby the party faith shall be declared and the party discipline enforced. The pith of the matter is simply this, that when those agencies are invested with an authority independent of

the will of the association in whose name they undertake
to speak, they become to that extent the organs of the
State itself, the repositories of official power. They are
then the governmental instruments whereby parties are
organized and regulated to the end that government itself
may be established or continued. What they do in that relation, they must do in submission to the mandates of
equality and liberty that bind officials everywhere. They
are not acting in matters of merely private concern like
the directors or agents of business corporations. They are
acting in matters of high public interest, matters intimate-
ly connected with the capacity of government to exercise
its functions unbrokenly and smoothly. Whether in given
circumstances parties or their committees are agencies of
government within the Fourteenth or the Fifteenth
Amendment is a question which this court will determine
for itself. It is not concluded upon such an inquiry by decisions rendered elsewhere. The test is not whether the
members of the Executive Committee are the representatives of the State in the strict sense in which an agent is
the representative of his principal. The test is whether
they are to be classified as representatives of the State to
such an extent and in such a sense that the great restraints
of the Constitution set limits to their action.

With the problem thus laid bare and its essentials exposed
to view, the case is seen to be ruled by *Nixon v. Herndon.*
Delegates of the State's power have discharged their official functions in such a way as to discriminate invidiously
between white citizens and black. The Fourteenth
Amendment, adopted as it was with special solicitude for
the equal protection of members of the Negro race, lays a
duty upon the court to level by its judgment these barriers of color.

The judgment below is reversed and the cause remanded [returned to the lower court] for further proceedings in conformity with this opinion.

PUBLIC TRANSPORTATION

Morgan v. Virginia

All persons who fail while on any motor vehicle carrier, to take and occupy the seats assigned to them by the driver, or who fail to obey the direction of the driver to change their seats from time to time as occasions require, pursuant to any lawful rule, regulation or custom in force as to the assigning of separate seats to white and colored persons, respectively, having been first advised of the fact of such regulation and requested to conform thereto, shall be deemed guilty of a misdemeanor.

The Virginia Segregated Bus Law

In the 1930's and '40's ten states, Alabama, Arkansas, Georgia, Louisiana, Mississippi, North Carolina, Oklahoma, South Carolina, Texas, and Virginia, enacted laws that required, under criminal penalties, the separation of white and colored passengers on both interstate and intrastate buses. Irene Morgan, a colored passenger traveling on an interstate bus trip from Gloucester County, Virginia, through the District of Columbia and on to Baltimore, Maryland, was ordered, while in Virginia, to yield her seat to a white passenger and move to the back of the bus. She refused. Mrs. Morgan was arrested, tried, and convicted of a violation of the Virginia Segregated Bus Law. The Supreme Court of Appeals of Virginia upheld her conviction. Mrs. Morgan's lawyer, Thurgood Marshall of the NAACP's Legal Defense and Education Fund, argued that the Constitution's Commerce Clause, Article I, Section 8, Clause 3, which says, "Congress shall have power . . . to regulate commerce . . . among the States," made the Virginia Law an interference with interstate commerce and thus an unconstitutional act. Irene Morgan appealed to the United States Supreme Court.

On June 3, 1946 Justice Stanley Reed announced the decision of the Court. The edited text follows.

THE MORGAN COURT

Chief Justice Harlan Fiske Stone
Appointed by President Coolidge
Served 1925 - 1946

Associate Justice Hugo Black
Appointed by President Franklin Roosevelt
Served 1937 - 1971

Associate Justice Stanley Reed
Appointed by President Franklin Roosevelt
Served 1938 - 1957

Associate Justice Felix Frankfurter
Appointed by President Franklin Roosevelt
Served 1939 - 1962

Associate Justice William O. Douglas
Appointed by President Franklin Roosevelt
Served 1939 - 1975

Associate Justice Frank Murphy
Appointed by President Franklin Roosevelt
Served 1940 - 1949

Associate Justice Robert Jackson
Appointed by President Franklin Roosevelt
Served 1941 - 1954

Associate Justice Wiley Rutledge
Appointed by President Franklin Roosevelt
Served 1943 - 1949

Associate Justice Harold Burton
Appointed by President Truman
Served 1945 - 1958

The unedited text of *Morgan v. Virginia* can be found on page 373, volume 328 of *United States Reports.*

MORGAN v. VIRGINIA
June 3, 1946

JUSTICE REED: This appeal brings to this Court the question of the constitutionality of an act of Virginia, which requires all passenger motor vehicle carriers, both interstate and intrastate, to separate without discrimination the white and colored passengers in their motor buses so that contiguous seats will not be occupied by persons of different races at the same time. A violation of the requirement of separation by the carrier is a misdemeanor. The driver or other person in charge is directed and required to increase or decrease the space allotted to the respective races as may be necessary or proper and may require passengers to change their seats to comply with the allocation. The operator's failure to enforce the provisions is made a misdemeanor.

These regulations were applied to an interstate passenger, this appellant [Morgan], on a motor vehicle then making an interstate run or trip. According to the statement of fact by the Supreme Court of Appeals of Virginia, [Morgan], who is a Negro, was traveling on a motor common carrier, operating under the above-mentioned statute, from Gloucester County, Virginia, through the District of Columbia, to Baltimore, Maryland, the destination of the bus. There were other passengers, both white and colored. On her refusal to accede to a request of the driver to move to a back seat, which was partly occupied by other colored passengers, so as to permit the seat that she vacated to be used by white passengers, a warrant was obtained and [Morgan] was arrested, tried and convicted of a violation of [the segregated bus provisions] of the Virginia Code. . . . [T]he conviction was affirmed [upheld] by the Supreme Court of Appeals of Virginia. The Court of Appeals interpreted the Virginia statute as applicable to [Morgan] since the statute "embraces all motor vehicles and all passengers, both interstate and intrastate." The Court of Appeals refused to accept [Morgan]'s contention that the statute applied was invalid as a delegation of legislative power to the carrier by a concurrent holding "that no power is delegated to the carrier to legislate. . . . The statute itself condemns the defendant's conduct as a violation of law and not the rule of the carrier." No complaint is made as to these interpretations of the Virginia statute by the Virginia court.

The errors of the Court of Appeals that are assigned and relied upon by [Morgan] are in form only two. The first is that the decision is repugnant to Clause 3, Section 8, Article I of the Constitution of the United States, and the second the holding that powers reserved to the states by the Tenth Amendment include the power to require an interstate motor passenger to occupy a seat restricted for the use of his race. Actually, the first question alone needs consideration for, if the statute unlawfully burdens interstate commerce, the reserved powers of the state will not validate it.

We think, as the Court of Appeals apparently did, that [Morgan] is a proper person to challenge the validity of this statute as a burden on commerce. If it is an invalid burden, the conviction under it would fail. The statute affects [Morgan] as well as the transportation company. Constitutional protection against burdens on commerce is for her benefit on a criminal trial for violation of the challenged statute.

This Court frequently must determine the validity of state statutes that are attacked as unconstitutional interferences with the national power over interstate commerce. This appeal presents that question as to a statute that compels racial segregation of interstate passengers in vehicles moving interstate.

The precise degree of a permissible restriction on state power cannot be fixed generally or indeed not even for one kind of state legislation, such as taxation or health or safety. There is a recognized abstract principle, however, that may be taken as a postulate for testing whether particular state legislation in the absence of action by Congress is beyond state power. This is that the state legislation is invalid if it unduly burdens that commerce in matters where uniformity is necessary - necessary in the constitutional sense of useful in accomplishing a permitted purpose. Where uniformity is essential for the functioning of commerce, a state may not interpose its local regulation. Too true it is that the principle lacks in precision. Although the quality of such a principle is abstract, its application to the facts of a situation created by the attempted enforcement of a statute brings about a specific determination as to whether or not the statute in question is a burden on commerce. Within the broad limits of the principle, the case[s] turn on their own facts.

In the field of transportation, there has been a series of decisions which hold that where Congress has not acted and although the state statute affects interstate commerce, a state may validly enact legislation which has predominantly only a local influence on the course of commerce. It is equally well settled that, even where Congress has not acted, state legislation or a final court order is invalid which materially affects interstate commerce. Because the Constitution puts the ultimate power to regulate commerce in Congress, rather than the states, the degree of state legislation's interference with that commerce may be weighed by federal courts to determine whether the burden makes the statute unconstitutional. The courts could not invalidate federal legislation for the same reason because Congress, within the limits of the Fifth Amendment, has authority to burden commerce if that seems to it a desirable means of accomplishing a permitted end.

This statute is attacked on the ground that it imposes undue burdens on interstate commerce. It is said by the Court of Appeals to have been passed in the exercise of the state's police power to avoid friction between the races. But this Court pointed out years ago "that a State cannot avoid the operation of this rule by simply invoking the convenient apologetics of the police power." Burdens upon commerce are those actions of a state which directly "impair the usefulness of its facilities for such traffic." That impairment, we think, may arise from other causes than costs or long delays. A burden may arise from a state statute which requires interstate passengers to order their movements on the vehicle in accordance with local rather than national requirements.

On [Morgan]'s journey, this statute required that she sit in designated seats in Virginia. Changes in seat designation might be made "at any time" during the journey when "necessary or proper for the comfort and convenience of passengers." This occurred in this instance. Upon such change of designation, the statute authorizes the operator of the vehicle to require, as he did here, "any passenger to change his or her seat as it may be necessary or proper." An interstate passenger must if necessary repeatedly shift seats while moving in Virginia to meet the seating requirements of the changing passenger group. On arrival at the District of Columbia line, [Morgan] would have had freedom to occupy any available seat and so to the end of her journey.

Interstate passengers traveling via motor buses between the north and south or the east and west may pass through Virginia on through lines in the day or in the night. The large buses approach the comfort of pullmans and have seats convenient for rest. On such interstate journeys the enforcement of the requirements for reseating would be disturbing.

[Morgan]'s argument, properly we think, includes facts bearing on interstate motor transportation beyond those immediately involved in this journey under the Virginia statutory regulations. To appraise the weight of the burden of the Virginia statute on interstate commerce, related statutes of other states are important to show whether there are cumulative effects which may make local regulation impracticable. Eighteen states, it appears, prohibit racial separation on public carriers. Ten require separation on motor carriers. Of these, Alabama applies specifically to interstate passengers with an exception for interstate passengers with through tickets from states without laws on separation of passengers. The language of the other acts, like this Virginia statute before the Court of Appeals' decision in this case, may be said to be susceptible to an interpretation that they do or do not apply to interstate passengers.

In states where separation of races is required in motor vehicles, a method of identification as white or colored must be employed. This may be done by definition. Any ascertainable Negro blood identifies a person as colored for purposes of separation in some states. In the other states which require the separation of the races in motor carriers, apparently no definition generally applicable or made for the purposes of the statute is given. Court definition or further legislative enactments would be required to clarify the line between the races. Obviously there may be changes by legislation in the definition.

The interferences to interstate commerce which arise from state regulation of racial association on interstate vehicles has long been recognized. Such regulation hampers freedom of choice in selecting accommodations. The recent changes in transportation brought about by the coming of automobiles does not seem of great significance in the problem. People of all races travel today more extensively than in 1878 when this Court first passed upon state regulation of racial segregation in commerce. The factual situation set out in preceding paragraphs emphasizes the soundness of this Court's early conclusion in *Hall v. DeCuir.*

The *DeCuir* case arose under a statute of Louisiana interpreted by the courts of that state and this Court to require public carriers "to give all persons travelling in that State, upon the public conveyances employed in such business, equal rights and privileges in all parts of the conveyance, without distinction or discrimination on account of race or color." Damages were awarded against Hall, the representative of the operator of a Mississippi river steamboat that traversed that river interstate from New Orleans to Vicksburg, for excluding in Louisiana the defendant . . . , a colored person, from a cabin reserved for whites. This Court reversed for reasons well stated in the words of Chief Justice Waite. As our previous discussion demonstrates, the transportation difficulties arising from a statute that requires commingling of the races, as in the *DeCuir* case, are increased by one that requires separation, as here. Other federal courts have looked upon racial separation statutes as applied to interstate passengers as burdens upon commerce.

In weighing the factors that enter into our conclusion as to whether this statute so burdens interstate commerce or so infringes the requirements of national uniformity as to be invalid, we are mindful of the fact that conditions vary between northern or western states such as Maine or Montana, with practically no colored population; industrial states such as Illinois, Ohio, New Jersey and Pennsylvania with a small, although appreciable, percentage of colored citizens; and the states of the deep south with percentages of from twenty-five to nearly fifty per cent colored, all with varying densities of the white and colored races in certain localities. Local efforts to promote amicable relations in difficult areas by legislative segregation in interstate transportation emerge from the latter racial distribution. As no state law can reach beyond its own border nor bar transportation of passengers across its boundaries, diverse seating requirements for the races in interstate journeys result. As there is no federal act dealing with the separation of races in interstate transportation, we must decide the validity of this Virginia statute on the challenge that it interferes with commerce, as a matter of balance between the exercise of the local police power and the need for national uniformity in the regulations for interstate travel. It seems clear to us that seating arrangements for the different races in interstate motor travel require a single, uniform rule to promote and protect national travel. Consequently, we hold the Virginia statute in controversy invalid. Reversed.

RACIALLY RESTRICTED HOUSING
Shelley v. Kraemer

[N]o part of said property or any portion thereof shall be, for the said term of fifty years, occupied by any person not of the Caucasian race, it being intended hereby to restrict the use of said property for the said period of time against the occupancy as owners or tenants of any portion of said property for resident or other purpose by people of the Negro or Mongolian Race.

The Labadie Avenue Covenant

On February 16, 1911 thirty white homeowners on Labadie Avenue in St. Louis, Missouri signed a private agreement to restrict home ownership and occupancy on their street to whites only. The "restricted street" comprised forty-seven parcels of land on the north and south sides of Labadie Avenue, between Taylor and Cora Avenues. The period of the Labadie Avenue Covenant, commonly known as a racially restrictive covenant, was fifty years.

Thirty-four years later, in August 1945 the Shelleys, a Negro couple, unaware of the existence of the covenant, purchased, through a real estate agent, one of the forty-seven restricted parcels on Labadie Avenue. In October 1945 the Labadie Avenue homeowners brought suit against the Shelleys, demanding the Missouri Courts enforce their restrictive covenant. A St. Louis Circuit Court, on a technicality, found for the Shelleys. The Missouri Supreme Court found for the homeowners. That Court held the racially restrictive Labadie Avenue Covenant violated no rights guaranteed by the Federal Constitution and ordered its enforcement. The Shelleys, asserting their Fourteenth Amendment right to equal protection, appealed to the United States Supreme Court.

On May 3, 1948 Chief Justice Fredrick Vinson announced the 6-0 (Justices Reed, Jackson, and Rutledge not taking part) decision of the Court. The edited text follows.

THE SHELLEY COURT

Chief Justice Fredrick Vinson
Appointed by President Truman
Served 1946 - 1953

Associate Justice Hugo Black
Appointed by President Franklin Roosevelt
Served 1937 - 1971

Associate Justice Stanley Reed
Appointed by President Franklin Roosevelt
Served 1938 - 1957

Associate Justice Felix Frankfurter
Appointed by President Franklin Roosevelt
Served 1939 - 1962

Associate Justice William O. Douglas
Appointed by President Franklin Roosevelt
Served 1939 - 1975

Associate Justice Frank Murphy
Appointed by President Franklin Roosevelt
Served 1940 - 1949

Associate Justice Robert Jackson
Appointed by President Franklin Roosevelt
Served 1941 - 1954

Associate Justice Wiley Rutledge
Appointed by President Franklin Roosevelt
Served 1943 - 1949

Associate Justice Harold Burton
Appointed by President Truman
Served 1945 - 1958

The unedited text of *Shelley v. Kraemer* can be found on page 1, volume 334 of *United States Reports.*

SHELLEY v. KRAEMER
May 3, 1948

CHIEF JUSTICE VINSON: [This case presents] for our consideration questions relating to the validity of court enforcement of private agreements, generally described as restrictive covenants, which have as their purpose the exclusion of persons of designated race or color from the ownership or occupancy of real property. Basic constitutional issues of obvious importance have been raised.

[This case] comes to this Court [from] the Supreme Court of Missouri. On February 16, 1911, thirty out of a total of thirty-nine owners of property fronting both sides of Labadie Avenue between Taylor Avenue and Cora Avenue in the city of St. Louis, signed an agreement, which was subsequently recorded, providing in part:

> ". . . the said property is hereby restricted to the use and occupancy for the term of Fifty (50) years from this date, so that it shall be a condition all the time and whether recited and referred to as [*sic*] not in subsequent conveyances and shall attach to the land as a condition precedent to the sale of the same, that hereafter no part of said property or any portion thereof shall be, for said term of Fifty years, occupied by any person not of the Caucasian race, it being intended hereby to restrict the use of said property for said period of time against the occupancy as owners or tenants of any portion of said property for resident or other purpose by people of the Negro or Mongolian Race."

The entire district described in the agreement included fifty-seven parcels of land. The thirty owners who signed the agreement held title to forty-seven parcels, including the particular parcel involved in this case. At the time the agreement was signed, five of the parcels in the district were owned by Negroes. One of those had been occupied by Negro families since 1882, nearly thirty years before the restrictive agreement was executed. The trial court found that owners of seven out of nine homes on the south side of Labadie Avenue, within the restricted district and "in the immediate vicinity" of the premises in question, had failed to sign the restrictive agreement in 1911. At the time this action was brought, four of the premises were occupied by Negroes, and had been so occupied for periods ranging from twenty-three to sixty-three years. A fifth parcel had been occupied by Negroes until a year before this suit was instituted.

On August 11, 1945, pursuant to a contract of sale, petitioners Shelley, who are Negroes, for valuable consideration received from one Fitzgerald a warranty deed to the parcel in question. The trial court found that [the Shelleys] had no actual knowledge of the restrictive agreement at the time of the purchase.

On October 9, 1945, [the Kraemers], as owners of other property subject to the terms of the restrictive covenant, brought suit in the Circuit Court of the city of St. Louis [asking] that [the Shelleys] be restrained from taking possession of the property and that judgment be entered divesting title out of [the Shelleys] and revesting title in the immediate grantor [Fitzgerald] or in such other person as the court should direct. The trial court denied the requested relief on the ground that the restrictive agreement, upon which [the Kraemers] based their action, had never become final and complete because it was the intention of the parties to that agreement that it was not to become effective until signed by all property owners in the district, and signatures of all the owners had never been obtained.

The Supreme Court of Missouri sitting *en banc* [with all members of the court participating] reversed and directed the trial court to grant the relief for which [the Kraemers] had prayed. That court held the agreement effective and concluded that enforcement of its provisions violated no rights guaranteed to [the Shelleys] by the Federal Constitution. At the time the court rendered its decision, [the Shelleys] were occupying the property in question.

. . . . [The Shelleys] have placed primary reliance on their contentions, first raised in the state courts, that judicial enforcement of the restrictive agreements in [this case] has violated rights guaranteed to [the Shelleys] by the Fourteenth Amendment of the Federal Constitution and Acts of Congress passed pursuant to that Amendment. Specifically, [the Shelleys] urge that they have been denied the equal protection of the laws, deprived of property without due process of law, and have been denied privileges and immunities of citizens of the United States. We pass to a consideration of those issues.

Whether the equal protection clause of the Fourteenth Amendment inhibits judicial enforcement by state courts of restrictive covenants based on race or color is a question which this Court has not heretofore been called upon to consider. Only two cases have been decided by this Court which in any way have involved the enforcement of such agreements. The first of these was the case of *Corrigan v. Buckley*. There, suit was brought in the courts of

the District of Columbia to enjoin [stop] a threatened violation of certain restrictive covenants relating to lands situated in the city of Washington. Relief was granted, and
the case was brought here on appeal. It is apparent that
that case, which had originated in the federal courts and
involved the enforcement of covenants on land located in
the District of Columbia, could present no issues under
the Fourteenth Amendment; for that Amendment by its
terms applies only to the States. . . . The only constitutional issue . . . raised in the lower courts, and hence the
only constitutional issue before this Court on appeal, was
the validity of the covenant agreements as such. This
Court concluded that since the inhibitions of the constitutional provisions invoked apply only to governmental action, as contrasted to action of private individuals, there
was no showing that the covenants, which were simply
agreements between private property owners, were invalid. Accordingly, the appeal was dismissed. . . .

The second of the cases involving racial restrictive covenants was *Hansberry v. Lee.* In that case, petitioners,
white property owners, were enjoined by the state courts
from violating the terms of a restrictive agreement. The
state Supreme Court had held petitioners bound by an earlier judicial determination, in litigation in which petitioners were not parties, upholding the validity of the restrictive agreement, although, in fact, the agreement had not
been signed by the number of owners necessary to make it
effective under state law. This Court reversed the judgment of the state Supreme Court upon the ground that petitioners had been denied due process of law. . . .

It is well, at the outset, to scrutinize the terms of the restrictive agreements involved in [this case]. . . . [T]he
covenant declares that no part of the affected property

shall be "occupied by any person not of the Caucasian race, it being intended hereby to restrict the use of said property . . . against the occupancy as owners or tenants of any portion of said property for resident or other purpose by people of the Negro or Mongolian Race." Not only does the restriction seek to proscribe [prohibit] use and occupancy of the affected properties by members of the excluded class, but as construed [interpreted] by the Missouri courts, the agreement requires that title of any person who uses his property in violation of the restriction shall be divested. . . .

It should be observed that [this covenant] do[es] not seek to proscribe any particular use of the affected properties. Use of the properties for residential occupancy, as such, is not forbidden. The restrictions . . . , rather, are directed toward a designated class of persons and seek to determine who may and who may not own or make use of the properties for residential purposes. The excluded class is defined wholly in terms of race or color; "simply that and nothing more."

It cannot be doubted that among the civil rights intended to be protected from discriminatory state action by the Fourteenth Amendment are the rights to acquire, enjoy, own and dispose of property. Equality in the enjoyment of property rights was regarded by the framers of that Amendment as an essential pre-condition to the realization of other basic civil rights and liberties which the Amendment was intended to guarantee. Thus, Section 1978 of the Revised Statutes, derived from Section 1 of the Civil Rights Act of 1866 which was enacted by Congress while the Fourteenth Amendment was also under consideration, provides:

"All citizens of the United States shall have the same right, in every State and Territory, as is enjoyed by white citizens thereof to inherit, purchase, lease, sell, hold, and convey real and personal property."

This Court has given specific recognition to the same principle.

It is likewise clear that restrictions on the right of occupancy of the sort sought to be created by the private agreements in these cases could not be squared with the requirements of the Fourteenth Amendment if imposed by state statute or local ordinance. We do not understand [the Kraemers] to urge the contrary. In the case of *Buchanan v. Warley,* a unanimous Court declared unconstitutional the provisions of a city ordinance which denied to colored persons the right to occupy houses in blocks in which the greater number of houses were occupied by white persons, and imposed similar restrictions on white persons with respect to blocks in which the greater number of houses were occupied by colored persons. During the course of the opinion in that case, this Court stated: "The Fourteenth Amendment and these statutes enacted in furtherance of its purpose operate to qualify and entitle a colored man to acquire property without state legislation discriminating against him solely because of color."

In *Harmon v. Tyler,* a unanimous court . . . declared invalid an ordinance which forbade any Negro to establish a home on any property in a white community or any white person to establish a home in a Negro community, "except on the written consent of a majority of the persons of the opposite race inhabiting such community or portion of the City to be affected."

The precise question before this Court in both the *Buchanan* and *Harmon* cases involved the rights of white sellers to dispose of their properties free from restrictions as to potential purchasers based on considerations of race or color. But that such legislation is also offensive to the rights of those desiring to acquire and occupy property and barred on grounds of race or color is clear, not only from the language of the opinion in *Buchanan v. Warley*, but from this Court's disposition of the case of *Richmond v. Deans*. There, a Negro, barred from the occupancy of certain property by the terms of an ordinance similar to that in the *Buchanan* case, sought injunctive relief [a court order] in the federal courts to enjoin the enforcement of the ordinance on the grounds that its provisions violated the terms of the Fourteenth Amendment. Such relief was granted, and this Court affirmed [upheld]. . . .

But the present [case], unlike those just discussed, do[es] not involve action by state legislatures or city councils. Here the particular patterns of discrimination and the areas in which the restrictions are to operate, are determined, in the first instance, by the terms of agreements among private individuals. Participation of the State consists in the enforcement of the restrictions so defined. The crucial issue with which we are here confronted is whether this distinction removes [this case] from the operation of the prohibitory provisions of the Fourteenth Amendment.

Since the decision of this Court in the *Civil Rights Cases*, the principle has become firmly embedded in our constitutional law that the action inhibited by the first section of the Fourteenth Amendment is only such action as may fairly be said to be that of the States. That Amendment erects no shield against merely private conduct, however discriminatory or wrongful.

We conclude, therefore, that the restrictive agreements standing alone cannot be regarded as violative of any rights guaranteed to [the Shelleys] by the Fourteenth Amendment. So long as the purposes of those agreements are effectuated by voluntary adherence to their terms, it would appear clear that there has been no action by the State and the provisions of the Amendment have not been violated.

But here there was more. [This is a case] in which the [purpose] of the [agreement was] secured only by judicial enforcement by state courts of the restrictive terms of the [agreement]. The [Kraemers] urge that judicial enforcement of private agreements does not amount to state action; or, in any event, the participation of the State is so attenuated in character as not to amount to state action within the meaning of the Fourteenth Amendment. Finally, it is suggested, even if the States in these cases may be deemed to have acted in the constitutional sense, their action did not deprive [the Shelleys] of rights guaranteed by the Fourteenth Amendment. We move to a consideration of these matters.

That the action of state courts and judicial officers in their official capacities is to be regarded as action of the State within the meaning of the Fourteenth Amendment, is a proposition which has long been established by decisions of this Court. That principle was given expression in the earliest cases involving the construction of the terms of the Fourteenth Amendment. Thus, in *Virginia v. Rives*, this Court stated: "It is doubtless true that a State may act through different agencies, either by its legislative, its executive, or its judicial authorities; and the prohibitions of the amendment extend to all action of the State denying equal protection of the laws, whether it be action by one of these agencies or by another." In *Ex parte Virginia*, the Court observed: "A State acts by its legislative, its executive, or its judicial authorities. It can act in no other way." In the *Civil Rights Cases*, this Court pointed out that the Amendment makes void "State action of every kind" which is inconsistent with the guaranties therein contained, and extends to manifestations of "State authority in the shape of laws, customs, or judicial or executive proceedings." Language to like effect is employed no less than eighteen times during the course of that opinion.

Similar expressions, giving specific recognition to the fact that judicial action is to be regarded as action of the State for the purposes of the Fourteenth Amendment, are to be found in numerous cases which have been more recently decided. In *Twining v. New Jersey*, the Court said: "The judicial act of the highest court of the State, in authoritatively construing [interpreting] and enforcing its laws, is the act of the State." In *Brinkerhoff-Faris Trust & Savings Co. v. Hill*, the Court, through Justice Brandeis, stated: "The federal guaranty of due process extends to state action through its judicial as well as through its legislative, executive or administrative branch of government." Further examples of such declarations in the opinions of this Court are not lacking.

One of the earliest applications of the prohibitions contained in the Fourteenth Amendment to action of state judicial officials occurred in cases in which Negroes had been excluded from jury service in criminal prosecutions by reason of their race or color. These cases demonstrate,

also, the early recognition by this Court that state action
in violation of the Amendment's provisions is equally repugnant to the constitutional commands whether directed
by state statute or taken by a judicial official in the absence of statute. Thus, in *Strauder v. West Virginia*, this
Court declared invalid a state statute restricting jury service to white persons as amounting to a denial of the equal
protection of the laws to the colored defendant in that
case. . . . [T]he Court in *Ex parte Virginia* held that a
similar discrimination imposed by the action of a state
judge denied rights protected by the Amendment, despite
the fact that the language of the state statute relating to
jury service contained no such restrictions.

The action of state courts in imposing penalties or depriving parties of other substantive rights without providing
adequate notice and opportunity to defend, has, of course,
long been regarded as a denial of the due process of law
guaranteed by the Fourteenth Amendment.

In numerous cases, this Court has reversed criminal convictions in state courts for failure of those courts to provide the essential ingredients of a fair hearing. Thus it
has been held that convictions obtained in state courts under the domination of a mob are void. Convictions obtained by coerced confessions, by the use of perjured testimony known by the prosecution to be such, or without the
effective assistance of counsel, have also been held to be
exertions of state authority in conflict with the fundamental rights protected by the Fourteenth Amendment.

But the examples of state judicial action which have been
held by this Court to violate the Amendment's commands
are not restricted to situations in which the judicial proceedings were found in some manner to be procedurally

unfair. It has been recognized that the action of state courts in enforcing a substantive common-law rule formulated by those courts, may result in the denial of rights guaranteed by the Fourteenth Amendment, even though the judicial proceedings in such cases may have been in complete accord, with the most rigorous conceptions of procedural due process. Thus, in *American Federation of Labor v. Swing*, enforcement by state courts of the common-law policy of the State, which resulted in the restraining of peaceful picketing, was held to be state action of the sort prohibited by the Amendment's guaranties of freedom of discussion. In *Cantwell v. Connecticut*, a conviction in a state court of the common-law crime of breach of the peace was, under the circumstances of the case, found to be a violation of the Amendment's commands relating to freedom of religion. In *Bridges v. California*, enforcement of the state's common-law rule relating to contempts by publication was held to be state action inconsistent with the prohibitions of the Fourteenth Amendment.

The short of the matter is that from the time of the adoption of the Fourteenth Amendment until the present, it has been the consistent ruling of this Court that the action of the States to which the Amendment has reference includes action of state courts and state judicial officials. Although, in construing the terms of the Fourteenth Amendment, differences have from time to time been expressed as to whether particular types of state action may be said to offend the Amendment's prohibitory provisions, it has never been suggested that state court action is immunized from the operation of those provisions simply because the act is that of the judicial branch of the state government.

Against this background of judicial construction, extending over a period of some three-quarters of a century, we are called upon to consider whether enforcement by state courts of the restrictive agreements in [this case] may be deemed to be the acts of those States; and, if so, whether that action has denied [the Shelleys] the equal protection of the laws which the Amendment was intended to insure.

We have no doubt that there has been state action in [this case] in the full and complete sense of the phrase. The undisputed facts disclose that [the Shelleys] were willing purchasers of properties upon which they desired to establish homes. The owners of the properties were willing sellers; and contracts of sale were accordingly consummated. It is clear that but for the active intervention of the state courts, supported by the full panoply of state power, [the Shelleys] would have been free to occupy the properties in question without restraint.

[This is not a case], as has been suggested, in which the [State has] merely abstained from action, leaving private individuals free to impose such discriminations as they see fit. Rather, [this is a case] in which the [State has] made available to such individuals the full coercive power of government to deny to [the Shelleys], on the grounds of race or color, the enjoyment of property rights in premises which [the Shelleys] are willing and financially able to acquire and which [Fitzgerald is] willing to sell. The difference between judicial enforcement and non-enforcement of the restrictive covenants is the difference to [the Shelleys] between being denied rights of property available to other members of the community and being accorded full enjoyment of those rights on an equal footing.

The enforcement of the restrictive agreements by the state courts in [this case] was directed pursuant to the common-law policy of the [State] as formulated by those courts in earlier decisions. . . . [E]nforcement of the covenant was directed in the first instance by the highest court of the State after the trial court had determined the agreement to be invalid for want of the requisite number of signatures. . . . The judicial action . . . bears the clear and unmistakable imprimatur of the State. We have noted that previous decisions of this Court have established the proposition that judicial action is not immunized from the operation of the Fourteenth Amendment simply because it is taken pursuant to the state's common-law policy. Nor is the Amendment ineffective simply because the particular pattern of discrimination, which the State has enforced, was defined initially by the terms of a private agreement. State action, as that phrase is understood for the purposes of the Fourteenth Amendment, refers to exertions of state power in all forms. And when the effect of that action is to deny rights subject to the protection of the Fourteenth Amendment, it is the obligation of this Court to enforce the constitutional commands.

We hold that in granting judicial enforcement of the restrictive agreements in [this case], the [State has] denied [the Shelleys] the equal protection of the laws and that, therefore, the action of the state courts cannot stand. We have noted that freedom from discrimination by the States in the enjoyment of property rights was among the basic objectives sought to be effectuated by the framers of the Fourteenth Amendment. That such discrimination has occurred in [this case] is clear. Because of the race or color of [the Shelleys] they have been denied rights of ownership or occupancy enjoyed as a matter of course by other citizens of different race or color. The Fourteenth

Amendment declares "that all persons, whether colored or white, shall stand equal before the laws of the States, and, in regard to the colored race, for whose protection the amendment was primarily designed, that no discrimination shall be made against them by law because of their color." Only recently this Court had occasion to declare that a state law which denied equal enjoyment of property rights to a designated class of citizens of specified race and ancestry, was not a legitimate exercise of the state's police power but violated the guaranty of the equal protection of the laws. Nor may the discriminations imposed by the state courts in [this case] be justified as proper exertions of state police power.

[Kraemer urges], however, that since the state courts stand ready to enforce restrictive covenants excluding white persons from the ownership or occupancy of property covered by such agreements, enforcement of covenants excluding colored persons may not be deemed a denial of equal protection of the laws to the colored persons who are thereby affected. This contention does not bear scrutiny. The parties have directed our attention to no case in which a court, state or federal, has been called upon to enforce a covenant excluding members of the white majority from ownership or occupancy of real property on grounds of race or color. But there are more fundamental considerations. The rights created by the first section of the Fourteenth Amendment are, by its terms, guaranteed to the individual. The rights established are personal rights. It is, therefore, no answer to [the Shelleys] to say that the courts may also be induced to deny white persons rights of ownership and occupancy on grounds of race or color. Equal protection of the laws is not achieved through indiscriminate imposition of inequalities.

Nor do we find merit in the suggestion that property owners who are parties to these agreements are denied equal protection of the laws if denied access to the courts to enforce the terms of restrictive covenants and to assert property rights which the state courts have held to be created by such agreements. The Constitution confers upon no individual the right to demand action by the State which results in the denial of equal protection of the laws to other individuals. And it would appear beyond question that the power of the State to create and enforce property interests must be exercised within the boundaries defined by the Fourteenth Amendment.

The problem of defining the scope of the restrictions which the Federal Constitution imposes upon exertions of power by the States has given rise to many of the most persistent and fundamental issues which this Court has been called upon to consider. That problem was foremost in the minds of the framers of the Constitution, and, since that early day, has arisen in a multitude of forms. The task of determining whether the action of a State offends constitutional provisions is one which may not be undertaken lightly. Where, however, it is clear that the action of the State violates the terms of the fundamental charter, it is the obligation of this Court so to declare.

The historical context in which the Fourteenth Amendment became a part of the Constitution should not be forgotten. Whatever else the framers sought to achieve, it is clear that the matter of primary concern was the establishment of equality in the enjoyment of basic civil and political rights and the preservation of those rights from discriminatory action on the part of the States based on considerations of race or color. Seventy-five years ago this Court announced that the provisions of the Amendment are to be construed with this fundamental purpose in mind. Upon full consideration, we have concluded that in [this case the State has] acted to deny [the Shelleys] the equal protection of the laws guaranteed by the Fourteenth Amendment. Having so decided, we find it unnecessary to consider whether [the Shelleys] have also been deprived of property without due process of law or denied privileges and immunities of citizens of the United States.

For the reasons stated, the judgment of the Supreme Court of Missouri . . . must be reversed.

PUBLIC ACCOMMODATIONS

The Heart Of Atlanta Motel Case

*All persons shall be entitled to the full and equal enjoy-
ment of the goods, services, facilities, privileges, advantages and accommodations of any place of public accommodation . . . without discrimination or segregation on the
ground of race, color, religion, or national origin.*

Discrimination In Places Of Public Accommodation
Title II, The Civil Rights Act of 1964

The Civil Rights Act of 1875 made acts of racial discrimination in public accommodation illegal. In 1883's *Civil
Rights Cases* (see Volume I) the Supreme Court struck
down as unconstitutional the antidiscrimination in public
accommodations provisions of the 1875 Act. The Court
held that the Fourteenth Amendment's Equal Protection
Clause did not give Congress the right to make acts of private discrimination illegal. Ninety years later the antidiscrimination in public accommodations provisions of Title
II of the Civil Rights Act of 1964 again made acts of racial discrimination in public accommodation illegal. This
time the legislation was based not on the Fourteenth
Amendment's Equal Protection Clause, but on the Constitution's Commerce Clause (Article 1, Section 8, Clause 3).

The Heart of Atlanta Motel, located in downtown Atlanta,
Georgia, refused accommodation to Negro guests for racial reasons. Under Title II of the Civil Rights Act of
1964 the owner of the motel, three-quarters of whose
guests were interstate travelers, was sued for practicing
racial discrimination in public accommodation. The owner attacked the constitutionality of the Act as a violation
of the Fifth and Thirteenth Amendments. A Federal District Court upheld its constitutionality and the owner appealed to the United States Supreme Court.

On December 14, 1964 Justice Tom Clark announced the
9-0 decision of the Court. The edited text follows.

THE HEART OF ATLANTA COURT

Chief Justice Earl Warren
Appointed by President Eisenhower
Served 1953 - 1969

Associate Justice Hugo Black
Appointed by President Franklin Roosevelt
Served 1937 - 1971

Associate Justice William O. Douglas
Appointed by President Franklin Roosevelt
Served 1939 - 1975

Associate Justice Tom Clark
Appointed by President Truman
Served 1949 - 1967

Associate Justice John M. Harlan
Appointed by President Eisenhower
Served 1955 - 1971

Associate Justice William Brennan
Appointed by President Eisenhower
Served 1956 - 1990

Associate Justice Potter Stewart
Appointed by President Eisenhower
Served 1958 - 1981

Associate Justice Byron White
Appointed by President Kennedy
Served 1962 - 1993

Associate Justice Arthur Goldberg
Appointed by President Kennedy
Served 1962 - 1965

The unedited text of *Heart of Atlanta Motel* is found on page 241, volume 379 of *United States Reports.*

HEART OF ATLANTA MOTEL v. UNITED STATES
December 14, 1964

JUSTICE CLARK: This [case] attack[s] the constitutionality of Title II of the Civil Rights Act of 1964. . . .

Appellant owns and operates the Heart of Atlanta Motel which has 216 rooms available to transient guests. The motel is located on Courtland Street, two blocks from downtown Peachtree Street. It is readily accessible to interstate highways 75 and 85 and state highways 23 and 41. [The motel] solicits patronage from outside the State of Georgia through various national advertising media, including magazines of national circulation; it maintains over 50 billboards and highway signs within the State, soliciting patronage for the motel; it accepts convention trade from outside Georgia and approximately 75% of its registered guests are from out of State. Prior to passage of the Act the motel had followed a practice of refusing to rent rooms to Negroes, and it alleged that it intended to continue to do so. In an effort to perpetuate that policy this suit was filed.

The [motel] contends that Congress in passing this Act exceeded its power to regulate commerce under Article I, Section 8, Clause 3, of the Constitution of the United States; that the Act violates the Fifth Amendment because [the motel] is deprived of the right to choose its customers and operate its business as it wishes, resulting in a taking of its liberty and property without due process of law and a taking of its property without just compensation; and, finally, that by requiring [the motel] to rent available rooms to Negroes against its will, Congress is subjecting it to involuntary servitude in contravention of the Thirteenth Amendment.

The appellees [the government] counter that the unavailability to Negroes of adequate accommodations interferes significantly with interstate travel, and that Congress, under the Commerce Clause, has power to remove such obstructions and restraints; that the Fifth Amendment does not forbid reasonable regulation and that consequential damage does not constitute a "taking" within the meaning of that amendment; that the Thirteenth Amendment claim fails because it is entirely frivolous to say that an amendment directed to the abolition of human bondage and the removal of widespread disabilities associated with slavery places discrimination in public accommodations beyond the reach of both federal and state law.

At the trial the [motel] offered no evidence ... ; however, [the government] proved the refusal of the motel to accept Negro transients after the passage of the Act. The District Court sustained [maintained] the constitutionality of the sections of the Act under attack and issued a permanent injunction [a court order stopping an act] on the counterclaim of the [government]. It restrained the [motel] from "[r]efusing to accept Negroes as guests in the motel by reason of their race or color" and from "[m]aking any distinction whatever upon the basis of race or color in the availability of the goods, services, facilities, privileges, advantages or accommodations offered or made available to the guests of the motel, or to the general public, within or upon any of the premises of the Heart of Atlanta Motel, Inc."

Congress first evidenced its interest in civil rights legislation in the Civil Rights Enforcement Act of April 9,

1866. There followed four Acts, with a fifth, the Civil Rights Act of March 1, 1875, culminating the series. In 1883 this Court struck down the public accommodations sections of the 1875 Act in the *Civil Rights Cases.* No major legislation in this field had been enacted by Congress for 82 years when the Civil Rights Act of 1957 became law. It was followed by the Civil Rights Act of 1960. Three years later, on June 19, 1963, the late President Kennedy called for civil rights legislation in a message to Congress to which he attached a proposed bill. Its stated purpose was

> "to promote the general welfare by eliminating discrimination based on race, color, religion, or national origin in . . . public accommodations through the exercise by Congress of the powers conferred upon it . . . to enforce the provisions of the fourteenth and fifteenth amendments, to regulate commerce among the several States, and to make laws necessary and proper to execute the powers conferred upon it by the Constitution."

Bills were introduced in each House of the Congress, embodying the President's suggestion, one in the Senate . . . and one in the House. . . . However, it was not until July 2, 1964, upon the recommendation of President Johnson, that the Civil Rights Act of 1964, here under attack, was finally passed.

After extended hearings each of these bills was favorably reported to its respective house. . . . Although each bill originally incorporated extensive findings of fact these were eliminated from the bills as they were reported. The House passed its bill in January 1964 and sent it to the Senate. Through a bipartisan coalition of Senators Humphrey and Dirksen, together with other Senators, a substitute was worked out in informal conferences. This substitute was adopted by the Senate and sent to the House where it was adopted without change. This expedited procedure prevented the usual report on the substitute bill in the Senate as well as a Conference Committee report ordinarily filed in such matters. Our only frame of reference as to the legislative history of the Act is, therefore, the hearings, reports and debates on the respective bills in each house.

The Act as finally adopted was most comprehensive, undertaking to prevent through peaceful and voluntary settlement discrimination in voting, as well as in places of accommodation and public facilities, federally secured programs and in employment. Since Title II is the only portion under attack here, we confine our consideration to those public accommodation provisions.

This Title is divided into seven sections beginning with Section 201(a) which provides that:

"All persons shall be entitled to the full and equal enjoyment of the goods, services, facilities, privileges, advantages, and accommodations of any place of public accommodation, as defined in this section, without discrimination or segregation on the ground of race, color, religion, or national origin."

There are listed in Section 201(b) four classes of business establishments, each of which "serves the public" and "is a place of public accommodation" within the meaning of Section 201(a) "if its operations affect commerce, or if discrimination or segregation by it is supported by State action." The covered establishments are:

"(1) any inn, hotel, motel, or other establishment which provides lodging to transient guests, other than an establishment located within a building which contains not more than five rooms for rent or hire and which is actually occupied by the proprietor of such establishment as his residence;

"(2) any restaurant, cafeteria . . . [not here involved];

"(3) any motion picture house . . . [not here involved];

"(4) any establishment . . . which is physically located within the premises of any establishment otherwise covered by this subsection, or . . . within the premises of which is physically located any such covered establishment . . . [not here involved]."

Section 201(c) defines the phrase "affect commerce" as applied to the above establishments. It first declares that "any inn, hotel, motel, or other establishment which provides lodging to transient guests" affects commerce *per se.* Restaurants, cafeterias, etc., in class two affect commerce only if they serve or offer to serve interstate travelers or if a substantial portion of the food which they serve or products which they sell have "moved in commerce." Motion picture houses and other places listed in class three affect commerce if they customarily present films, performances, etc., "which move in commerce." And the establishments listed in class four affect commerce if they are within, or include within their own premises, an establishment "the operations of which affect commerce." Private clubs are excepted under certain conditions.

Section 201(d) declares that "discrimination or segregation" is supported by state action when carried on under color of any law, statute, ordinance, regulation or any custom or usage required or enforced by officials of the State or any of its subdivisions.

In addition, Section 202 affirmatively declares that all persons "shall be entitled to be free, at any establishment or place, from discrimination or segregation of any kind on the ground of race, color, religion, or national origin, if such discrimination or segregation is or purports to be required by any law, statute, ordinance, regulation, rule, or order of a State or any agency or political subdivision thereof."

Finally, Section 203 prohibits the withholding or denial, etc., of any right or privilege secured by Section 201 and Section 202 or the intimidation, threatening or coercion of any person with the purpose of interfering with any such right or the punishing, etc., of any person for exercising or attempting to exercise any such right.

The remaining sections of the Title are remedial ones for violations of any of the previous sections. . . . The Attorney General may bring suit where he has "reasonable cause to believe that any person or group of persons is engaged in a pattern or practice of resistance to the full enjoyment of any of the rights secured by this title, and that the pattern or practice is of such a nature and is intended to deny the full exercise of the rights herein described. . . ."

A person aggrieved may bring suit, in which the Attorney General may be permitted to intervene. Thirty days' written notice before filing any such action must be given to the appropriate authorities of a State or subdivision the law of which prohibits the act complained of and which has established an authority which may grant relief therefrom. In States where such condition does not exist the court after a case is filed may refer it to the Community Relations Service which is established under Title X of the Act. This Title establishes such service in the Department of Commerce, provides for a Director to be appointed by the President with the advice and consent of the Senate and grants it certain powers, including the power to hold hearings, with reference to matters coming to its attention by reference from the court or between communities and persons involved in disputes arising under the Act.

It is admitted that the operation of the motel brings it within the provisions of Section 201(a) of the Act and that [the motel] refused to provide lodging for transient Negroes because of their race or color and that it intends to continue that policy unless restrained.

The sole question posed is, therefore, the constitutionality of the Civil Rights Act of 1964 as applied to these facts. The legislative history of the Act indicates that Congress based the Act on Section 5 and the Equal Protection Clause of the Fourteenth Amendment as well as its power to regulate interstate commerce under Article I, Section 8, Clause 3, of the Constitution.

The Senate Commerce Committee made it quite clear that the fundamental object of Title II was to vindicate "the deprivation of personal dignity that surely accompanies

denials of equal access to public establishments." At the
same time, however, it noted that such an objective has
been and could be readily achieved "by congressional action based on the commerce power of the Constitution."
Our study of the legislative record, made in the light of
prior cases, has brought us to the conclusion that Congress
possessed ample power in this regard, and we have therefore not considered the other grounds relied upon. This is
not to say that the remaining authority upon which it acted was not adequate, a question upon which we do not
pass, but merely that since the commerce power is sufficient for our decision here we have considered it alone.
Nor is Section 201(d) or Section 202, having to do with
state action, involved here and we do not pass upon either
of those sections.

In light of our ground for decision, it might be well at the
outset to discuss the *Civil Rights Cases*, which declared
provisions of the Civil Rights Act of 1875 unconstitutional. We think that decision inapposite, and without prece-
dential [based on previous cases] value in determining the
constitutionality of the present Act. Unlike Title II of the
present legislation, the 1875 Act broadly proscribed
[forbade] discrimination in "inns, public conveyances on
land or water, theaters, and other places of public amuse-
ment," without limiting the categories of affected businesses to those impinging upon interstate commerce. In
contrast, the applicability of Title II is carefully limited to
enterprises having a direct and substantial relation to the
interstate flow of goods and people, except where state action is involved. Further, the fact that certain kinds of
businesses may not in 1875 have been sufficiently involved in interstate commerce to warrant bringing them
within the ambit of the commerce power is not necessarily dispositive of the same question today. Our populace

had not reached its present mobility, nor were facilities, goods and services circulating as readily in interstate commerce as they are today. Although the principles which we apply today are those first formulated by Chief Justice Marshall in *Gibbons v. Ogden*, the conditions of transportation and commerce have changed dramatically, and we must apply those principles to the present state of commerce. The sheer increase in volume of interstate traffic alone would give discriminatory practices which inhibit travel a far larger impact upon the Nation's commerce than such practices had on the economy of another day. Finally, there is language in the *Civil Rights Cases* which indicates that the Court did not fully consider whether the 1875 Act could be sustained [maintained] as an exercise of the commerce power. Though the Court observed that "no one will contend that the power to pass it was contained in the Constitution before the adoption of the last three amendments [Thirteenth, Fourteenth, and Fifteenth]," the Court went on specifically to note that the Act was not "conceived" in terms of the commerce power and expressly pointed out:

"Of course, these remarks [as to lack of congressional power] do not apply to those cases in which Congress is clothed with direct and plenary powers of legislation over the whole subject, accompanied with an express or implied denial of such power to the States, as in the regulation of commerce with foreign nations, among the several States, and with the Indian tribes. . . . In these cases Congress has power to pass laws for regulating the subjects specified in every detail, and the conduct and transactions of individuals in respect thereof."

Since the commerce power was not relied on by the Government and was without support in the record it is understandable that the Court narrowed its inquiry and excluded the Commerce Clause as a possible source of power. In any event, it is clear that such a limitation renders the opinion devoid of authority for the proposition that the Commerce Clause gives no power to Congress to regulate discriminatory practices now found substantially to affect interstate commerce. We, therefore, conclude that the *Civil Rights Cases* have no relevance to the basis of decision here where the Act explicitly relies upon the commerce power, and where the record is filled with testimony of obstructions and restraints resulting from the discriminations found to be existing. We now pass to that phase of the case.

While the Act as adopted carried no congressional findings the record of its passage through each house is replete with evidence of the burdens that discrimination by race or color places upon interstate commerce. This testimony included the fact that our people have become increasingly mobile with millions of people of all races traveling from State to State; that Negroes in particular have been the subject of discrimination in transient accommodations, having to travel great distances to secure the same; that often they have been unable to obtain accommodations and have had to call upon friends to put them up overnight, and that these conditions had become so acute as to require the listing of available lodging for Negroes in a special guidebook which was itself "dramatic testimony to the difficulties" Negroes encounter in travel. These exclusionary practices were found to be nationwide, the Under Secretary of Commerce testifying that there is "no question that this discrimination in the North still exists to a large degree" and in the West and Midwest as well. This testimony indicated a qualitative as well as quantitative effect on interstate travel by Negroes. The former was the obvious impairment of the Negro traveler's pleasure and convenience that resulted when he continually was uncertain of finding lodging. As for the latter, there was evidence that this uncertainty stemming from racial discrimination had the effect of discouraging travel on the part of a substantial portion of the Negro community. This was the conclusion not only of the Under Secretary of Commerce but also of the Administrator of the Federal Aviation Agency who wrote the Chairman of the Senate Commerce Committee that it was his "belief that air commerce is adversely affected by the denial to a substantial segment of the traveling public of adequate and desegregated public accommodations." We shall not burden this opinion with further details since the voluminous testimony presents overwhelming evidence that discrimination by hotels and motels impedes interstate travel.

The power of Congress to deal with these obstructions depends on the meaning of the Commerce Clause. Its meaning was first enunciated 140 years ago by the great Chief Justice John Marshall in *Gibbons v. Ogden*, in these words:

"The subject to be regulated is commerce; and . . . to ascertain the extent of the power, it becomes necessary to settle the meaning of the word. The counsel for the appellee would limit it to traffic, to buying and selling, or the interchange of commodities . . . but it is something more: it is intercourse . . . between nations, and parts of nations, in all its branches, and is regulated by prescribing rules for carrying on that intercourse. . . .

"To what commerce does this power extend? The
constitution informs us, to commerce 'with foreign nations, and among the several States, and
with the Indian tribes.'

"It has, we believe, been universally admitted,
that these words comprehend every species of
commercial intercourse. . . . No sort of trade can
be carried on . . . to which this power does not extend. . . .

"The subject to which the power is next applied,
is to commerce 'among the several States.' The
word 'among' means intermingled. . . .

". . . [I]t may very properly be restricted to that
commerce which concerns more States than one.
. . . The genius and character of the whole government seem to be, that its action is to be applied to all the . . . internal concerns [of the Na-
tion] which affect the States generally; but not to
those which are completely within a particular
State, which do not affect other States, and with
which it is not necessary to interfere, for the purpose of executing some of the general powers of
the government. . . .

"We are now arrived at the inquiry - What is this
power?

"It is the power to regulate; that is, to prescribe
the rule by which commerce is to be governed.
This power, like all others vested in Congress, is
complete in itself, may be exercised to its utmost
extent, and acknowledges no limitations, other

Heart of Atlanta Motel v. United States 181

than are prescribed in the constitution. . . . If, as has always been understood, the sovereignty of Congress . . . is plenary as to those objects [specified in the Constitution], the power over commerce . . . is vested in Congress as absolutely as it would be in a single government, having in its constitution the same restrictions on the exercise of the power as are found in the constitution of the United States. The wisdom and the discretion of Congress, their identity with the people, and the influence which their constituents possess at elections, are, in this, as in many other instances, as that, for example, of declaring war, the sole restraints on which they have relied, to secure them from its abuse. They are the restraints on which the people must often rely solely, in all representative governments."

In short, the determinative test of the exercise of power by the Congress under the Commerce Clause is simply whether the activity sought to be regulated is "commerce which concerns more States than one" and has a real and substantial relation to the national interest. Let us now turn to this facet of the problem.

That the "intercourse" of which the Chief Justice spoke included the movement of persons through more States than one was settled as early as 1849, in the *Passenger Cases*, where Justice McLean stated: "That the transportation of passengers is a part of commerce is not now an open question." Again in 1913 Justice McKenna, speaking for the Court, said: "Commerce among the States, we have said, consists of intercourse and traffic between their citizens, and includes the transportation of persons and property." And only four years later in 1917 in *Caminetti v. United States*, Justice Day held for the Court:

"The transportation of passengers in interstate commerce, it has long been settled, is within the regulatory power of Congress, under the commerce clause of the Constitution, and the authority of Congress to keep the channels of interstate commerce free from immoral and injurious uses has been frequently sustained, and is no longer open to question."

Nor does it make any difference whether the transportation is commercial in character. In *Morgan v. Virginia*, Justice Reed observed as to the modern movement of persons among the States:

"The recent changes in transportation brought about by the coming of automobiles [do] not seem of great significance in the problem. People of all races travel today more extensively than in 1878 when this Court first passed upon state regulation of racial segregation in commerce. [It but] emphasizes the soundness of this Court's early conclusion in *Hall v. DeCuir*."

The same interest in protecting interstate commerce which led Congress to deal with segregation in interstate carriers and the white-slave traffic has prompted it to extend the exercise of its power to gambling; to criminal enterprises; to deceptive practices in the sale of products; to fraudulent security transactions; to misbranding of drugs; to wages and hours; to members of labor unions; to crop control; to discrimination against shippers; to the protection of small business from injurious price cutting; to resale price maintenance; to professional football; and to racial discrimination by owners and managers of terminal restaurants.

That Congress was legislating against moral wrongs in many of these areas rendered its enactments no less valid. In framing Title II of this Act Congress was also dealing with what it considered a moral problem. But that fact does not detract from the overwhelming evidence of the disruptive effect that racial discrimination has had on commercial intercourse. It was this burden which empowered Congress to enact appropriate legislation, and, given this basis for the exercise of its power, Congress was not restricted by the fact that the particular obstruction to interstate commerce with which it was dealing was also deemed a moral and social wrong.

It is said that the operation of the motel here is of a purely local character. But, assuming this to be true, "[i]f it is interstate commerce that feels the pinch, it does not matter how local the operation which applies the squeeze." As Chief Justice Stone put it in *United States v. Darby:*

> "The power of Congress over interstate commerce is not confined to the regulation of commerce among the states. It extends to those activities intrastate which so affect interstate commerce or the exercise of the power of Congress over it as to make regulation of them appropriate means to the attainment of a legitimate end, the exercise of the granted power of Congress to regulate interstate commerce."

Thus the power of Congress to promote interstate commerce also includes the power to regulate the local inci-

dents thereof, including local activities in both the States
of origin and destination, which might have a substantial
and harmful effect upon that commerce. One need only
examine the evidence which we have discussed above to
see that Congress may - as it has - prohibit racial discrimination by motels serving travelers, however "local" their
operations may appear.

Nor does the Act deprive [the motel] of liberty or property under the Fifth Amendment. The commerce power invoked here by the Congress is a specific and plenary
[broad] one authorized by the Constitution itself. The
only questions are: (1) whether Congress had a rational
basis for finding that racial discrimination by motels affected commerce, and (2) if it had such a basis, whether
the means it selected to eliminate that evil are reasonable
and appropriate. If they are, [the motel] has no "right" to
select its guests as it sees fit, free from governmental regulation.

There is nothing novel about such legislation. Thirty-two
States now have it on their books either by statute or executive order and many cities provide such regulation.
Some of these Acts go back fourscore years. It has been
repeatedly held by this Court that such laws do not violate
the Due Process Clause of the Fourteenth Amendment.
Perhaps the first such holding was in the *Civil Rights
Cases* themselves, where Justice Bradley for the Court in-
ferentially found that innkeepers, "by the laws of all the
States, so far as we are aware, are bound, to the extent of
their facilities, to furnish proper accommodation to all un-
objectionable persons who in good faith apply for them."

As we have pointed out, 32 States now have such provisions and no case has been cited to us where the attack on

a state statute has been successful, either in federal or state courts. Indeed, in some cases the Due Process and Equal Protection Clause objections have been specifically discarded in this Court. As a result the constitutionality of such state statutes stands unquestioned. "The authority of the Federal Government over interstate commerce does not differ," it was held in *United States v. Rock Royal Co-op*, "in extent or character from that retained by the states over intrastate commerce."

It is doubtful if in the long run [the motel] will suffer economic loss as a result of the Act. Experience is to the contrary where discrimination is completely obliterated as to all public accommodations. But whether this be true or not is of no consequence since this Court has specifically held that the fact that a "member of the class which is regulated may suffer economic losses not shared by others . . . has never been a barrier" to such legislation. Likewise in a long line of cases this Court has rejected the claim that the prohibition of racial discrimination in public accommodations interferes with personal liberty. Neither do we find any merit in the claim that the Act is a taking of property without just compensation. The cases are to the contrary.

We find no merit in the remainder of [the motel]'s contentions, including that of "involuntary servitude." As we have seen, 32 States prohibit racial discrimination in public accommodations. These laws but codify the common-law innkeeper rule which long predated the Thirteenth Amendment. It is difficult to believe that the Amendment was intended to abrogate [annul] this principle. Indeed, the opinion of the Court in the *Civil Rights Cases* is to the contrary as we have seen, it having noted with approval the laws of "all the States" prohibiting discrimina-

tion. We could not say that the requirements of the Act
in this regard are in any way "akin to African slavery."

We, therefore, conclude that the action of the congress in
the adoption of the Act as applied here to a motel which
concededly serves interstate travelers is within the power
granted it by the Commerce Clause of the Constitution, as
interpreted by this Court for 140 years. It may be argued
that Congress could have pursued other methods to eliminate the obstructions it found in interstate commerce
caused by racial discrimination. But this is a matter of
policy that rests entirely with the Congress not with the
courts. How obstructions in commerce may be removed -
what means are to be employed - is within the sound and
exclusive discretion of the Congress. It is subject only to
one caveat - that the means chosen by it must be reasonably adapted to the end permitted by the Constitution. We
cannot say that its choice here was not so adapted. The
Constitution requires no more. Affirmed [upheld].

INTERRACIAL MARRIAGE

Loving v. Virginia

If any white person intermarry with a colored person, or any colored person intermarry with a white person, he shall be guilty of a felony and shall be punished by confinement in the penitentiary for not less than one nor more than five years.

The Virginia Racial Integrity Act

In 1924 the Commonwealth of Virginia adopted the Racial Integrity Act, which criminalized interracial marriage. Sixteen states enacted similar antimiscegenation laws. In June 1958 two Virginia citizens, Richard Perry Loving, a "white person," and Mildred Jeter, a "colored person," crossed over the state line into the District of Columbia to marry. Returning to Virginia, Richard and Mildred Loving set up their household in Caroline County. In January 1959 the Lovings were tried in a Caroline County Court for both leaving the state to marry and marrying, violating two provisions of the Racial Integrity Act, a felony. The Lovings, who under the laws of Virginia were not legally married, pled guilty. Each was sentenced to one year in the penitentiary. Their sentences were then suspended on the condition that they leave Virginia and not return together for twenty-five years.

In November 1963 the Lovings, then residents of the District of Columbia, petitioned the Virginia Courts to throw out the guilty judgments against them on the grounds that the Racial Integrity Act violated their civil rights under the Equal Protection and Due Process Clauses of the Fourteenth Amendment. In March 1966 the Virginia Supreme Court of Appeals upheld the constitutionality of the Racial Integrity Act and affirmed their sentences. The Lovings appealed to the United States Supreme Court.

On June 12, 1967 Chief Justice Earl Warren announced the 9-0 decision of the Court. The edited text follows.

THE LOVING COURT

Chief Justice Earl Warren
Appointed by President Eisenhower
Served 1953 - 1969

Associate Justice Hugo Black
Appointed by President Franklin Roosevelt
Served 1937 - 1971

Associate Justice William O. Douglas
Appointed by President Franklin Roosevelt
Served 1939 - 1975

Associate Justice Tom Clark
Appointed by President Truman
Served 1949 - 1967

Associate Justice John M. Harlan
Appointed by President Eisenhower
Served 1955 - 1971

Associate Justice William Brennan
Appointed by President Eisenhower
Served 1956 - 1990

Associate Justice Potter Stewart
Appointed by President Eisenhower
Served 1958 - 1981

Associate Justice Byron White
Appointed by President Kennedy
Served 1962 - 1993

Associate Justice Abe Fortas
Appointed by President Lyndon Johnson
Served 1965 - 1969

The unedited text of *Loving v. Virginia* can be found on page 1, volume 388 of *United States Reports.*

LOVING v. VIRGINIA
June 12, 1967

CHIEF JUSTICE WARREN: This case presents a constitutional question never addressed by this Court: whether a statutory scheme adopted by the State of Virginia to prevent marriages between persons solely on the basis of racial classifications violates the Equal Protection and Due Process Clauses of the Fourteenth Amendment. For reasons which seem to us to reflect the central meaning of those constitutional commands, we conclude that these statutes cannot stand consistently with the Fourteenth Amendment.

In June 1958, two residents of Virginia, Mildred Jeter, a Negro woman, and Richard Loving, a white man, were married in the District of Columbia pursuant to its laws. Shortly after their marriage, the Lovings returned to Virginia and established their marital abode in Caroline County. At the October Term, 1958, the Circuit Court of Caroline County, a grand jury issued an indictment charging the Lovings with violating Virginia's ban on interracial marriages. On January 6, 1959, the Lovings pleaded guilty to the charge and were sentenced to one year in jail; however, the trial judge suspended the sentence for a period of 25 years on the condition that the Lovings leave the State and not return to Virginia together for 25 years. He stated in an opinion that:

"Almighty God created the races white, black, yellow, malay and red, and he placed them on separate continents. And but for the interference with his arrangement there would be no cause for such marriages. The fact that he separated the races shows that he did not intend for the races to mix."

After their convictions, the Lovings took up residence in the District of Columbia. On November 6, 1963, they filed a motion [a request for a ruling] in the state trial court to vacate [throw out] the judgment and set aside the sentence on the ground that the statutes which they had violated were repugnant to the Fourteenth Amendment. The motion not having been decided by October 28, 1964, the Lovings instituted a class action [suit by a group of people with similar characteristics] in the United States District Court for the Eastern District of Virginia requesting that a three-judge court be convened to declare the Virginia antimiscegenation statutes unconstitutional and to enjoin [stop] state officials from enforcing their convictions. On January 22, 1965, the state trial judge denied the motion to [throw out] the sentences, and the Lovings [appealed] to the Supreme Court of Appeals of Virginia. On February 11, 1965, the three-judge District Court continued [postponed] the case to allow the Lovings to present their constitutional claims to the highest state court.

The Supreme Court of Appeals upheld the constitutionality of the antimiscegenation statutes and, after modifying the sentence, affirmed [upheld] the convictions. The Lovings appealed this decision, and we [agreed to hear the case].

The two statutes under which [the Lovings] were convicted and sentenced are part of a comprehensive statutory scheme aimed at prohibiting and punishing interracial marriages. The Lovings were convicted of violating Section 20-58 of the Virginia Code:

"*Leaving State to evade law.* If any white person and colored person shall go out of this State, for the purpose of being married, and with the intention of returning, and be married out of it, and afterwards return to and reside in it, cohabiting as man and wife, they shall be punished as provided in Section 20-59, and the marriage shall be governed by the same law as if it had been solemnized in this State. The fact of their cohabitation here as man and wife shall be evidence of their marriage."

Section 20-59, which defines the penalty for miscegenation, provides:

"*Punishment for marriage.* If any white person intermarry with a colored person, or any colored person intermarry with a white person, he shall be guilty of a felony and shall be punished by confinement in the penitentiary for not less than one nor more than five years."

Other central provisions in the Virginia statutory scheme are Section 20-57, which automatically voids all marriages between "a white person and a colored person" without any judicial proceeding, and Sections 20-54 and 1-14 which, respectively, define "white persons" and "colored persons and Indians" for purposes of the statutory prohibitions. The Lovings have never disputed in the course of this litigation that Mrs. Loving is a "colored person" or that Mr. Loving is a "white person" within the meanings given those terms by the Virginia Statutes.

Virginia is now one of 16 States which prohibit and punish marriages on the basis of racial classifications. Penal-

ties for miscegenation arose as an incident to slavery and
have been common in Virginia since the colonial period.
The present statutory scheme dates from the adoption of
the Racial Integrity Act of 1924, passed during the period
of extreme nativism which followed the end of the First
World War. The central features of this Act, and current
Virginia law, are the absolute prohibition of a "white person" marrying other than another "white person," a prohibition against issuing marriage licenses until the issuing
official is satisfied that the applicants' statements as to
their race are correct, certificates of "racial composition"
to be kept by both local and state registrars, and the carrying forward of earlier prohibitions against racial intermarriage.

In upholding the constitutionality of these provisions in
the decision [of the court] below, the Supreme Court of
Appeals of Virginia referred to its 1955 decision in *Naim
v. Naim*. . . . In' *Naim*, the state court concluded that the
State's legitimate purposes were "to preserve the racial integrity of its citizens," and to prevent "the corruption of
blood," "a mongrel breed of citizens," and "the obliteration
of racial pride," obviously an endorsement of the doctrine
of White Supremacy. The court also reasoned that marriage has traditionally been subject to state regulation
without federal intervention, and, consequently, the regulation of marriage should be left to exclusive state control
by the Tenth Amendment.

While the state court is no doubt correct is asserting that
marriage is a social relation subject to the State's police
power, the State does not contend in its argument before
this Court that its powers to regulate marriage are unlimited notwithstanding the commands of the Fourteenth
Amendment. . . . Instead, the State argues that the mean-

ing of the Equal Protection Clause, as illuminated by the statements of the Framers, is only that state penal laws containing an interracial element as part of the definition of the offense must apply equally to whites and Negroes in the sense that members of each race are punished to the same degree. Thus, the State contends that, because its miscegenation statutes punish equally both the white and the Negro participants in an interracial marriage, these statutes, despite their reliance on racial classifications, do not constitute an invidious discrimination based upon race. The second argument advanced by the State . . . is that, if the Equal Protection Clause does not outlaw miscegenation statutes because of their reliance on racial classifications, the question of constitutionality would thus become whether there was any rational basis for a State to treat interracial marriages differently from other marriages. On this question, the State argues, the scientific evidence is substantially in doubt and, consequently, this Court should defer to the wisdom of the state legislature in adopting its policy of discouraging interracial marriages.

Because we reject the notion that the mere "equal application" of a statute containing racial classifications is enough to remove the classifications from the Fourteenth Amendment's proscription of all invidious racial discriminations, we do not accept the State's contention that these statutes should be upheld if there is any possible basis for concluding that they serve a rational purpose. The mere fact of equal application does not mean that our analysis of these statutes should follow the approach we have taken in cases involving no racial discrimination where the Equal Protection Clause has been arrayed against a statute discriminating between the kinds of advertising which may be displayed on trucks in New York City, or an exemption in Ohio's ad valorem tax for merchandise owned by a nonresident in a storage warehouse. In these cases, involving distinctions not drawn according to race, the Court has merely asked whether there is any rational foundation for the discriminations, and has deferred to the wisdom of the state legislatures. In [this case], however, we deal with statutes containing racial classifications, and the fact of equal application does not immunize the statute from the very heavy burden of justification which the Fourteenth Amendment has traditionally required of state statutes drawn according to race.

The State argues that statements in the Thirty-ninth congress about the time of the passage of the Fourteenth Amendment indicate that the Framers did not intend the Amendment to make unconstitutional state miscegenation laws. Many of the statements alluded to by the State concern the debates over the Freedman's Bureau Bill, which President [Andrèw] Johnson vetoed, and the Civil Rights Act of 1866, enacted over his veto. While these statements have some relevance to the intention of Congress in submitting the Fourteenth Amendment, it must be understood that they pertained to the passage of specific statutes and not to the broader, organic purpose of a constitutional amendment. As for the various statements directly concerning the Fourteenth Amendment, we have said in connection with a related problem, that although these historical sources "cast some light" they are not sufficient to resolve the problem; "[a]t best, they are inconclusive. The most avid proponents of the post-War Amendments undoubtedly intended them to remove all legal distinctions among 'all persons born or naturalized in the United States.' Their opponents, just as certainly, were antagonistic to both the letter and the spirit of the Amendments and wished them to have the most limited effect." We

have rejected the proposition that the debates in the
Thirty-ninth congress or in the state legislatures which
ratified the Fourteenth Amendment supported the theory
advanced by the State, that the requirement of equal protection of the laws is satisfied by penal laws defining offenses based on racial classifications so long as white and
Negro participants in the offense were similarly punished.

The State finds support for its "equal application" theory
in the decision of the Court in *Pace v. Alabama.* In that
case, the Court upheld a conviction under an Alabama
statute forbidding adultery or fornication between a white
person and a Negro which imposed a greater penalty than
that of a statute proscribing similar conduct by members
of the same race. The Court reasoned that the statute
could not be said to discriminate against Negroes because
the punishment for each participant in the offense was
the same. However, as recently as the 1964 Term, in re-
jecting the reasoning of that case, we stated "*Pace* represents a limited view of the Equal Protection Clause which
has not withstood analysis in the subsequent decisions of
this Court." As we there demonstrated, the Equal Protection Clause requires the consideration of whether the classifications drawn by any statute constitute an arbitrary
and invidious discrimination. The clear and central purpose of the Fourteenth Amendment was to eliminate all
official state sources of invidious racial discrimination in
the States.

There can be no question but that Virginia's miscegenation statutes rest solely upon distinctions drawn according
to race. The statutes proscribe generally accepted conduct
if engaged in by members of different races. Over the
years, this Court has consistently repudiated
"[d]istinctions between citizens solely because of their an-

cestry" as being "odious to a free people whose institutions are founded upon the doctrine of equality." At the very least, the Equal Protection Clause demands that racial classifications, especially suspect in criminal statutes, be subjected to the "most rigid scrutiny," and, if they are ever to be upheld, they must be shown to be necessary to the accomplishment of some permissible state objective, independent of the racial discrimination which it was the object of the Fourteenth Amendment to eliminate. Indeed, two members of this Court have already stated that they "cannot conceive of a valid legislative purpose . . . which makes the color of a person's skin the test of whether his conduct is a criminal offense."

There is patently no legitimate overriding purpose independent of invidious racial discrimination which justifies this classification. The fact that Virginia prohibits only interracial marriages involving white persons demonstrates that the racial classifications must stand on their own justification, as measures designed to maintain White Supremacy. We have consistently denied the constitutionality of measures which restrict the rights of citizens on account of race. There can be no doubt that restricting the freedom to marry solely because of racial classifications violates the central meaning of the Equal Protection Clause.

These statutes also deprive the Lovings of liberty without due process of law in violation of the Due Process Clause of the Fourteenth Amendment. The freedom to marry has long been recognized as one of the vital personal rights essential to the orderly pursuit of happiness by free men.

Marriage is one of the "basic civil rights of man," fundamental to our very existence and survival. To deny this fundamental freedom on so unsupportable a basis as the racial classifications embodied in these statutes, classifications so directly subversive of the principle of equality at the heart of the Fourteenth Amendment, is surely to deprive all the State's citizens of liberty without due process of law. The Fourteenth Amendment requires that the freedom of choice to marry not be restricted by invidious racial discriminations. Under our Constitution, the freedom to marry, or not marry, a person of another race resides with the individual and cannot be infringed by the State.

These convictions must be reversed.

It is so ordered.

AFFIRMATIVE ACTION

The Regents of the University of California v. Allan Bakke

No person in the United States shall, on the ground of race, color, or national origin, be excluded from participation in, be denied the benefits of, or be subjected to discrimination under any program or activity receiving Federal financial assistance.

Title VI, The Civil Rights Act of 1964

The Medical School of the University of California at Davis accepted only 100 applicants each year. In 1973 a Special Admissions Program reserved 16 seats for minority applicants. Minority applicants were defined as: "Blacks," "Chicanos," "Asians," and "American Indians." Minority applicants could compete for all 100 openings; non-minorities could compete for only 84. The stated purposes of the Program were to (1) increase the number of traditionally disfavored minorities in medical schools, (2) counter the effects of societal discrimination, (3) increase the number of minority physicians practicing in underserved communities, and (4) create an ethnically diverse student body.

Allan Bakke, a white male, applied twice to the Medical School. He was denied admission twice despite test scores superior to minority applicants accepted under the Special Admissions Program. Bakke filed suit in state court claiming that the Special Admissions Program operated as a racially discriminatory quota, which was prohibited by the Fourteenth Amendment's Equal Protection Clause and the Civil Rights Act of 1964. The California Supreme Court held the Special Admissions Program unconstitutional and ordered Bakke admitted to Medical School. The University appealed to the U.S. Supreme Court.

On June 28, 1978 Justice Lewis Powell announced the 5-4 decision of the Court. The edited text follows.

THE BAKKE COURT

Chief Justice Warren Burger
Appointed by President Nixon
Served 1969 - 1986

Associate Justice William Brennan
Appointed by President Eisenhower
Served 1956 - 1990

Associate Justice Potter Stewart
Appointed by President Eisenhower
Served 1958 - 1981

Associate Justice Byron White
Appointed by President Kennedy
Served 1962 - 1993

Associate Justice Thurgood Marshall
Appointed by President Lyndon Johnson
Served 1967 - 1991

Associate Justice Harry Blackmun
Appointed by President Nixon
Served 1970 -

Associate Justice Lewis Powell
Appointed by President Nixon
Served 1971 - 1987

Associate Justice William Rehnquist
Appointed Associate Justice by President Nixon
Appointed Chief Justice by President Regan
Served 1971 -

Associate Justice John Paul Stevens
Appointed by President Ford
Served 1975 -

The unedited text of *University of California v. Bakke* is
found on page 265, volume 438 of *United States Reports.*

UNIVERSITY OF CALIFORNIA v. BAKKE
June 28, 1978

JUSTICE POWELL: This case presents a challenge to the special admissions program of the petitioner, the Medical School of the University of California at Davis, which is designed to assure the admission of a specified number of students from certain minority groups. The Superior Court of California sustained [maintained] respondent [Bakke]'s challenge, holding that [the University of California]'s program violated the California Constitution, Title VI of the Civil Rights Act of 1964, and the Equal Protection Clause of the Fourteenth Amendment. The court enjoined petitioner [prevented the University] from considering [Bakke]'s race or the race of any other applicant in making admissions decisions. It refused, however, to order [Bakke]'s admission to the Medical School, holding that he had not carried his burden of proving that he would have been admitted but for the constitutional and statutory violations. The Supreme Court of California affirmed [upheld] those portions of the trial court's judgment declaring the special admissions program unlawful and [prevented the University] from considering the race of any applicant. It . . . directed the trial court to order [Bakke's] admission.

The Medical School of the University of California at Davis opened in 1968 with an entering class of 50 students. In 1971, the size of the entering class was increased to 100 students, a level at which it remains. No admissions program for disadvantaged or minority students existed when the school opened, and the first class contained three Asians but no blacks, no Mexican-Americans, and no American Indians. Over the next two years, the faculty devised a special admissions program to increase the representation of "disadvantaged" students in each Medical School class. The special program consisted of a separate admissions system operating in coordination with the regular admissions process.

Under the regular admissions procedure, a candidate could submit his application to the Medical School beginning in July of the year preceding the academic year for which admission was sought. Because of the large number of applications, the admissions committee screened each one to select candidates for further consideration. Candidates whose overall undergraduate grade point averages fell below 2.5 on a scale of 4.0 were summarily rejected. About one out of six applicants was invited for a personal interview. Following the interviews, each candidate was rated on a scale of 1 to 100 by his interviewers and four other members of the admissions committee. The rating embraced the interviewers' summaries, the candidate's overall grade point average, grade point average in science courses, scores on the Medical College Admissions Test (MCAT), letters of recommendation, extracurricular activities, and other biographical data. The ratings were added together to arrive at each candidate's "benchmark" score. Since five committee members rated each candidate in 1973, a perfect score was 500; in 1974, six members rated each candidate, so that a perfect score was 600. The full committee then reviewed the file and scores of each applicant and made offers of admission on a "rolling" basis. The chairman was responsible for placing names on the waiting list. They were not placed in strict numerical order; instead, the chairman had discretion to include persons with "special skills."

The special admissions program operated with a separate committee, a majority of whom were members of minority groups. On the 1973 application form, candidates were asked to indicate whether they wished to be considered as "economically and/or educationally disadvantaged" applicants; on the 1974 form the question was whether they wished to be considered as members of a "minority group," which the Medical School apparently viewed as "Blacks," "Chicanos," "Asians," and "American Indians." If these questions were answered affirmatively, the application was forwarded to the special admission committee. No formal definition of "disadvantaged" was ever produced, but the chairman of the special committee screened each application to see whether it reflected economic or educational deprivation. Having passed this initial hurdle, the applications then were rated by the special committee in a fashion similar to that used by the general admissions committee, except that special candidates did not have to meet the 2.5 grade point average cutoff applied to regular applicants. About one-fifth of the total number of special applicants were invited for interviews in 1973 and 1974. Following each interview, the special committee assigned each special applicant a benchmark score. The special committee then presented its top choices to the general admissions committee. The latter did not rate or compare the special candidates against the general applicants, but could reject recommended special candidates for failure to meet course requirements or other specific deficiencies. The special committee continued to recommend special applicants until a number prescribed by faculty vote were admitted. While the overall class size was still 50, the prescribed number was 8; in 1973 and 1974, when the class size had doubled to 100, the prescribed number of special admissions also doubled, to 16.

From the year of the increase in class size - 1971 - through 1974, the special program resulted in the admission of 21 black students, 30 Mexican-Americans, and 12 Asians, for a total of 63 minority students. Over the same period, the regular admissions program produced 1 black, 6 Mexican-Americans, and 37 Asians, for a total of 44 minority students. Although disadvantaged whites applied to the special program in large numbers, none received an offer of admission through that process. Indeed, in 1974, the special committee explicitly considered only "disadvantaged" special applicants who were members of one of the designated minority groups.

Allan Bakke is a white male who applied to the Davis Medical School in both 1973 and 1974. In both years Bakke's application was considered under the general admissions program, and he received an interview. His 1973 interview was with Dr. Theodore C. West, who considered Bakke "a very desirable applicant to [the] medical school." Despite a strong benchmark score of 468 out of 500, Bakke was rejected. His application had come late in the year, and no applicants in the general admissions process with scores below 470 were accepted after Bakke's application was completed. There were four special admissions slots unfilled at that time, however, for which Bakke was not considered. After his 1973 rejection, Bakke wrote to Dr. George H. Lowrey, Associate Dean and Chairman of the Admissions Committee, protesting that the special admissions program operated as a racial and ethnic quota.

Bakke's 1974 application was completed early in the year. His student interviewer gave him an overall rating of 94, finding him "friendly, well tempered, conscientious and delightful to speak with." His faculty interviewer was, by coincidence, the same Dr. Lowrey to whom he had written in protest of the special admissions program. Dr. Lowrey found Bakke "rather limited in his approach" to the problems of the medical profession and found disturbing Bakke's "very definite opinions which were based more on his personal viewpoints than upon a study of the total problem." Dr. Lowrey gave Bakke the lowest of his six ratings, an 86; his total was 549 out of 600. Again, Bakke's application was rejected. In neither year did the chairman of the admissions committee, Dr. Lowrey, exercise his discretion to place Bakke on the waiting list. In both years, applicants were admitted under the special program with grade point averages, MCAT scores, and benchmark scores significantly lower than Bakke's.

After the second rejection, Bakke filed . . . suit in the Superior Court of California. He sought . . . relief compelling his admission to the Medical School. He alleged that the Medical School's special admissions program operated to exclude him from the school on the basis of his race, in violation of his rights under the Equal Protection Clause of the Fourteenth Amendment . . . the California Constitution, and . . . Title VI of the Civil Rights Act of 1964. The University cross-complained for a declaration that its special admissions program was lawful. The trial court found that the special program operated as a racial quota, because minority applicants in the special program were rated only against one another, and 16 places in the class of 100 were reserved for them. Declaring that the University could not take race into account in making admissions decisions, the trial court held the challenged program violative of the Federal Constitution, the State Constitution, and Title VI. The court refused to order Bakke's admission, however, holding that he had failed to carry his burden of proving that he would have been admitted but for the existence of the special program.

Bakke appealed from the portion of the trial court judgment denying him admission, and the University appealed from the decision that its special admissions program was unlawful and the order enjoining it from considering race in the processing of applications. The Supreme Court of California transferred the case directly from the trial court, "because of the importance of the issues involved." The California court accepted the findings of the trial court with respect to the University's program. Because the special admissions program involved a racial classification, the Supreme Court held itself bound to apply strict scrutiny. It then turned to the goals the University presented as justifying the special program. Although the court agreed that the goals of integrating the medical profession and increasing the number of physicians willing to serve members of minority groups were compelling state interests, it concluded that the special admissions program was not the least intrusive means of achieving those goals. Without passing on the state constitutional or the federal statutory grounds cited in the trial court's judgment, the California court held that the Equal Protection Clause of the Fourteenth Amendment required that "no applicant may be rejected because of his race, in favor of another who is less qualified, as measured by standards applied without regard to race."

Turning to Bakke's appeal, the court ruled that since Bakke had established that the University had discriminated against him on the basis of his race, the burden of proof shifted to the University to demonstrate that he would not have been admitted even in the absence of the special admissions program. The court analogized Bakke's situation to that of a plaintiff under Title VII of the Civil Rights Act of 1964. On this basis, the court initially ordered a remand [return to the lower court] for the pur-

pose of determining whether, under the newly allocated
burden of proof, Bakke would have been admitted to either the 1973 or the 1974 entering class in the absence of
the special admissions program. In its petition for rehear-
ing below, however, the University conceded its inability
to carry that burden. The California court thereupon
amended its opinion to direct that the trial court enter
judgment ordering Bakke's admission to the Medical
School. That order was stayed pending review in this
Court. We granted [review] to consider the important
constitutional issue....

The language of [Section] 601 [of the Civil Rights Act of
1964], like that of the Equal Protection Clause, is majestic
in its sweep:

> "No person in the United States shall, on the
> ground of race, color, or national origin, be ex-
> cluded from participation in, be denied the bene-
> fits of, or be subjected to discrimination under
> any program or activity receiving Federal finan-
> cial assistance."

The concept of "discrimination," like the phrase "equal
protection of the laws," is susceptible of varying interpretations, for as Justice Holmes declared, "[a] word is not a
crystal, transparent and unchanged, it is the skin of a living thought and may vary greatly in color and content according to the circumstances and the time in which it is
used." We must, therefore, seek whatever aid is available
in determining the precise meaning of the statute before
us. Examination of the voluminous legislative history of
Title VI reveals a congressional intent to halt federal
funding of entities that violate a prohibition of racial discrimination similar to that of the Constitution. Although

isolated statements of various legislators, taken out of context, can be marshaled in support of the proposition that [Section] 601 enacted a purely colorblind scheme, without regard to the reach of the Equal Protection Clause, these comments must be read against the background of both the problem that Congress was addressing and the broader view of the statute that emerges from a full examination of the legislative debates.

The problem confronting Congress was discrimination against Negro citizens at the hands of recipients of federal moneys. Indeed, the colorblindness pronouncements . . . generally occur in the midst of extended remarks dealing with the evils of segregation in federally funded programs. Over and over again, proponents of the bill detailed the plight of Negroes seeking equal treatment in such programs. There simply was no reason for Congress to consider the validity of hypothetical preferences that might be accorded minority citizens; the legislators were dealing with the real and pressing problem of how to guarantee those citizens equal treatment.

In addressing that problem, supporters of Title VI repeatedly declared that the bill enacted constitutional principles. For example, Representative Celler, the Chairman of the House Judiciary Committee and floor manager of the legislation in the House, emphasized this in introducing the bill:

> "The bill would offer assurance that hospitals financed by Federal money would not deny adequate care to Negroes. It would prevent abuse of food distribution programs whereby Negroes have been known to be denied food surplus supplies when white persons were given such food.

"It would assure Negroes the benefits now accorded only white students in programs of high[er] education financed by Federal funds. It would, in short, *assure the existing right to equal treatment* in the enjoyment of Federal funds. It would not destroy any rights of private property or freedom of association."

Other sponsors shared Representative Celler's view that Title VI embodied constitutional principles.

In the Senate, Senator Humphrey declared that the purpose of Title VI was "to insure that Federal funds are spent in accordance with the Constitution and the moral sense of the Nation." Senator Ribicoff agreed that Title VI embraced the constitutional standard: "Basically, there is a constitutional restriction against discrimination in the use of federal funds; and Title VI simply spells out the procedure to be used in enforcing that restriction." Other Senators expressed similar views.

Further evidence of the incorporation of a constitutional standard into Title VI appears in the repeated refusals of the legislation's supporters precisely to define the term "discrimination. Opponents sharply criticized this failure, but proponents of the bill merely replied that the meaning of "discrimination" would be made clear by reference to the Constitution or other existing law. For example, Senator Humphrey noted the relevance of the Constitution:

"As I have said, the bill has a simple purpose. That purpose is to give fellow citizens - Negroes - the same rights and opportunities that white people take for granted. This is no more than what was preached by the prophets, and by Christ Himself. It is no more than what our Constitution guarantees."

In view of the clear legislative intent, Title VI must be held to proscribe [forbid] only those racial classifications that would violate the Equal Protection Clause or the Fifth Amendment.

[The University] does not deny that decisions based on race or ethnic origin by faculties and administrations of state universities are reviewable under the Fourteenth Amendment. For his part, [Bakke] does not argue that all racial or ethnic classifications are *per se* [inherently] invalid. The parties do disagree as to the level of judicial scrutiny to be applied to the special admissions program. [The University] argues that the court below erred in applying strict scrutiny, as this inexact term has been applied in our cases. That level of review, [the University] asserts, should be reserved for classifications that disadvantage "discrete and insular minorities." [Bakke], on the other hand, contends that the California court correctly rejected the notion that the degree of judicial scrutiny accorded a particular racial or ethnic classification hinges upon membership in a discrete and insular minority and duly recognized that the "rights established [by the Fourteenth Amendment] are personal rights."

En route to this crucial battle over the scope of judicial review, the parties fight a sharp preliminary action over the proper characterization of the special admissions program. [The University] prefers to view it as establishing a "goal" of minority representation in the Medical School. [Bakke], echoing the courts below, labels it a racial quota.

This semantic distinction is beside the point: The special admissions program is undeniably a classification based on race and ethnic background. To the extent that there existed a pool of at least minimally qualified minority applicants to fill the 16 special admissions seats, white applicants could compete only for 84 seats in the entering class, rather than the 100 open to minority applicants. Whether this limitation is described as a quota or a goal, it is a line drawn on the basis of race and ethnic status.

The guarantees of the Fourteenth Amendment extend to all persons. Its language is explicit: "No State shall . . . deny to any person within its jurisdiction the equal protection of the laws." It is settled beyond question that the "rights created by the first section of the Fourteenth Amendment are, by its terms, guaranteed to the individual. The rights established are personal rights." The guarantee of equal protection cannot mean one thing when applied to one individual and something else when applied to a person of another color. If both are not accorded the same protection, then it is not equal.

Nevertheless, [the University of California] argues that the court below erred in applying strict scrutiny to the special admissions program because white males, such as [Bakke], are not a "discrete and insular minority" requiring extraordinary protection from the majoritarian political process. This rationale, however, has never been invoked in our decisions as a prerequisite to subjecting racial or ethnic distinctions to strict scrutiny. Nor has this Court held that discreteness and insularity constitute necessary preconditions to a holding that a particular classification is invidious. These characteristics may be relevant in deciding whether or not to add new types of classifications to the list of "suspect" categories or whether a par-

ticular classification survives close examination. Racial
and ethnic classifications, however, are subject to stringent
examination without regard to these additional characteristics. We declared as much in the first cases explicitly to
recognize racial distinctions as suspect:

> "Distinctions between citizens solely because of
> their ancestry are by their very nature odious to a
> free people whose institutions are founded upon
> the doctrine of equality."

> "[A]ll legal restrictions which curtail the civil
> rights of a single racial group are immediately
> suspect. That is not to say that all such restric-
> tions are unconstitutional. It is to say that courts
> must subject them to the most rigid scrutiny."

The Court has never questioned the validity of those pronouncements. Racial and ethnic distinctions of any sort
are inherently suspect and thus call for the most exacting
judicial examination.

This perception of racial and ethnic distinctions is rooted
in our Nation's constitutional and demographic history.
The Court's initial view of the Fourteenth Amendment
was that its "one pervading purpose" was "the freedom of
the slave race, the security and firm establishment of that
freedom, and the protection of the newly-made freeman
and citizen from the oppressions of those who had formerly exercised dominion over him." The Equal Protection Clause, however, was "[v]irtually strangled in infancy
by post-civil-war judicial reactionism." It was relegated to
decades of relative [disuse] while the Due Process Clause
of the Fourteenth Amendment, after a short germinal period, flourished as a cornerstone in the Court's defense of

property and liberty of contract. In that cause, the Fourteenth Amendment's "one pervading purpose" was dis-
placed. It was only as the era of substantive due process
came to a close that the Equal Protection Clause began to
attain a genuine measure of vitality.

By that time it was no longer possible to peg the guarantees of the Fourteenth Amendment to the struggle for
equality of one racial minority. During the dormancy of
the Equal Protection Clause, the United States had become
a Nation of minorities. Each had to struggle - and to
some extent struggles still - to overcome the prejudices
not of a monolithic majority, but of a "majority" composed of various minority groups of whom it was said -
perhaps unfairly in many cases - that a shared characteris-
tic was a willingness to disadvantage other groups. As the
Nation filled with the stock of many lands, the reach of
the Clause was gradually extended to all ethnic groups
seeking protection from official discrimination. The
guarantees of equal protection, said the Court in *Yick Wo,*
"are universal in their application, to all persons within
the territorial jurisdiction, without regard to any differences of race, of color, or of nationality; and the equal
protection of the laws is a pledge of the protection of
equal laws."

Although many of the Framers of the Fourteenth Amendment conceived of its primary function as bridging the
vast distance between members of the Negro race and the
white "majority," the Amendment itself was framed in
universal terms, without reference to color, ethnic origin,
or condition of prior servitude. As this Court recently remarked in interpreting the 1866 Civil Rights Act to extend to claims of racial discrimination against white persons, "the 39th Congress was intent upon establishing in

the federal law a broader principle than would have been necessary simply to meet the particular and immediate plight of the newly freed Negro slaves." And that legislation was specifically broadened in 1870 to ensure that "all persons," not merely "citizens," would enjoy equal rights under the law. Indeed, it is not unlikely that among the Framers were many who would have applauded a reading of the Equal Protection Clause that states a principle of universal application and is responsive to the racial, ethnic, and cultural diversity of the Nation.

Over the past 30 years, this Court has embarked upon the crucial mission of interpreting the Equal Protection Clause with the view of assuring to all persons "the protection of equal laws" in a Nation confronting a legacy of slavery and racial discrimination. Because the landmark decisions in this area arose in response to the continued exclusion of Negroes from the mainstream of American society, they could be characterized as involving discrimination by the "majority" white race against the Negro minority. But they need not be read as depending upon that characterization for their results. It suffices to say that "[o]ver the years, this Court has consistently repudiated '[d]istinctions between citizens solely because of their ancestry' as being 'odious to a free people whose institutions are founded upon the doctrine of equality.'"

[The University] urges us to adopt for the first time a more restrictive view of the Equal Protection Clause and hold that discrimination against members of the white "majority" cannot be suspect if its purpose can be characterized as "benign." The clock of our liberties, however, cannot be turned back to 1868. It is far too late to argue that the guarantee of equal protection to *all* persons permits the recognition of special wards entitled to a degree of protection greater than that accorded others. "The Fourteenth Amendment is not directed solely against discrimination due to a 'two-class theory' - that is, based upon differences between 'white' and Negro."

Once the artificial line of a "two-class theory" of the Fourteenth Amendment is put aside, the difficulties entailed in varying the level of judicial review according to a perceived "preferred" status of a particular racial or ethnic minority are intractable. The concepts of "majority" and "minority" necessarily reflect temporary arrangements and political judgments. As observed above, the white "majority" itself is composed of various minority groups, most of which can lay claim to a history of prior discrimination at the hands of the State and private individuals. Not all of these groups can receive preferential treatment and corresponding judicial tolerance of distinctions drawn in terms of race and nationality, for then the only "majority" left would be a new minority of white Anglo-Saxon Protestants. There is no principled basis for deciding which groups would merit "heightened judicial solicitude" and which would not. Courts would be asked to evaluate the extent of the prejudice and consequent harm suffered by various minority groups. Those whose societal injury is thought to exceed some arbitrary level of tolerability then would be entitled to preferential classifications at the expense of individuals belonging to other groups. Those classifications would be free from exacting judicial scrutiny. As these preferences began to have their desired effect, and the consequences of past discrimination were undone, new judicial rankings would be necessary. The kind of variable sociological and political analysis necessary to produce such rankings simply does not lie within the judicial competence - even if they otherwise were politically feasible and socially desirable.

Moreover, there are serious problems of justice connected with the idea of preference itself. First, it may not always be clear that a so-called preference is in fact benign. Courts may be asked to validate burdens imposed upon individual members of a particular group in order to advance the group's general interest. Nothing in the Constitution supports the notion that individuals may be asked to suffer otherwise impermissible burdens in order to enhance the societal standing of their ethnic groups. Second, preferential programs may only reinforce common stereotypes holding that certain groups are unable to achieve success without special protection based on a factor having no relationship to individual worth. Third, there is a measure of inequity in forcing innocent persons in [Bakke]'s position to bear the burdens of redressing grievances not of their making.

By hitching the meaning of the Equal Protection Clause to these transitory considerations, we would be holding, as a constitutional principle, that judicial scrutiny of classifications touching on racial and ethnic background may vary with the ebb and flow of political forces. Disparate constitutional tolerance of such classifications well may serve to exacerbate racial and ethnic antagonisms rather than alleviate them. Also, the mutability of a constitutional principle, based upon shifting political and social judgments, undermines the chances for consistent application of the Constitution from one generation to the next, a critical feature of its coherent interpretation. In expounding the Constitution, the Court's role is to discern "principles sufficiently absolute to give them roots throughout the community and continuity over significant periods of time, and to lift them above the level of the pragmatic political judgments of a particular time and place."

If it is the individual who is entitled to judicial protection against classifications based upon his racial or ethnic background because such distinctions impinge upon personal rights, rather than the individual only because of his membership in a particular group, then constitutional standards may be applied consistently. Political judgments regarding the necessity for the particular classification may be weighed in the constitutional balance, but the standard of justification will remain constant. This is as it should be, since those political judgments are the product of rough compromise struck by contending groups within the democratic process. When they touch upon an individual's race or ethnic background, he is entitled to a judicial determination that the burden he is asked to bear on that basis is precisely tailored to serve a compelling governmental interest. The Constitution guarantees that right to every person regardless of his background.

[The University] contends that on several occasions this Court has approved preferential classifications without applying the most exacting scrutiny. Most of the cases upon which [the University] relies are drawn from three areas: school desegregation, employment discrimination, and sex discrimination. Each of the cases cited presented a situation materially different from the facts of this case.

The school desegregation cases are inapposite. . . . The employment discrimination cases also do not advance [the University]'s cause. . . . Nor is [their] view as to the applicable standard supported by the fact that gender-based classifications are not subjected to this level of scrutiny. . . .

We have held that in "order to justify the use of a suspect classification, a State must show that its purpose or inter-

est is both constitutionally permissible and substantial,
and that its use of the classification is 'necessary . . . to the
accomplishment' of its purpose or the safeguarding of its
interest." The special admissions program purports to
serve the purposes of: (i) "reducing the historic deficit of
traditionally disfavored minorities in medical schools and
in the medical profession"; (ii) countering the effects of
societal discrimination; (iii) increasing the number of
physicians who will practice in communities currently underserved; and (iv) obtaining the educational benefits that
flow from an ethnically diverse student body. It is necessary to decide which, if any, of these purposes is substantial enough to support the use of a suspect classification.

If [the University]'s purpose is to assure within its student
body some specified percentage of a particular group
merely because of its race or ethnic origin, such a preferential purpose must be rejected not as unsubstantial but as
facially invalid. Preferring members of any one group
for no reason other than race or ethnic origin is discrimination for its own sake. This the Constitution forbids.

The State certainly has a legitimate and substantial interest in ameliorating, or eliminating where feasible, the disa-
bling effects of identified discrimination. The line of
school desegregation cases, commencing with *Brown*, at-
tests to the importance of this state goal and the commitment of the judiciary to affirm all lawful means toward
its attainment. In the school cases, the States were required by court order to redress the wrongs worked by
specific instances of racial discrimination. That goal was
far more focused than the remedying of the effects of
"societal discrimination," an amorphous concept of injury
that may be ageless in its reach into the past.

We have never approved a classification that aids persons perceived as members of relatively victimized groups at the expense of other innocent individuals in the absence of judicial, legislative, or administrative findings of constitutional or statutory violations. After such findings have been made, the governmental interest in preferring members of the injured groups at the expense of others is substantial, since the legal rights of the victims must be vindicated. In such a case, the extent of the injury and the consequent remedy will have been judicially, legislatively, or administratively defined. Also, the remedial action usually remains subject to continuing oversight to assure that it will work the least harm possible to other innocent persons competing for the benefit. Without such findings of constitutional or statutory violations, it cannot be said that the government has any greater interest in helping one individual than in refraining from harming another. Thus, the government has no compelling justification for inflicting such harm.

[The University] does not purport to have made, and is in no position to make, such findings. Its broad mission is education, not the formulation of any legislative policy or the adjudication of particular claims of illegality. For reasons similar to those stated [earlier in] this opinion, isolated segments of our vast governmental structures are not competent to make those decisions, at least in the absence of legislative mandates and legislatively determined criteria. Before relying upon these sorts of findings in establishing a racial classification, a governmental body must have the authority and capability to establish, in the record, that the classification is responsive to identified discrimination. Lacking this capability, [the University] has not carried its burden of justification on this issue.

Hence, the purpose of helping certain groups whom the faculty of the Davis Medical School perceived as victims of "societal discrimination" does not justify a classification that imposes disadvantages upon persons like [Bakke], who bear no responsibility for whatever harm the beneficiaries of the special admissions program are thought to have suffered. To hold otherwise would be to convert a remedy heretofore reserved for violations of legal rights into a privilege that all institutions throughout the Nation could grant at their pleasure to whatever groups are perceived as victims of societal discrimination. That is a step we have never approved.

[The University] identifies, as another purpose of its program, improving the delivery of health-care services to communities currently underserved. It may be assumed that in some situations a State's interest in facilitating the health care of its citizens is sufficiently compelling to support the use of a suspect classification. But there is virtually no evidence in the record indicating that [the University]'s special admissions program is either needed or geared to promote that goal. The court below addressed this failure of proof:

> "The University concedes it cannot assure that minority doctors who entered under the program, all of whom expressed an 'interest' in practicing in a disadvantaged community, will actually do so. It may be correct to assume that some of them will carry out this intention, and that it is more likely they will practice in minority communities than the average white doctor. Nevertheless, there are more precise and reliable ways to identify applicants who are genuinely interested in the medical problems of minorities than by

race. An applicant of whatever race who has demonstrated his concern for disadvantaged minorities in the past and who declares that practice in such a community is his primary professional goal would be more likely to contribute to alleviation of the medical shortage than one who is chosen entirely on the basis of race and disadvantage. In short, there is no empirical data to demonstrate that any one race is more selflessly socially oriented or by contrast that another is more selfishly acquisitive."

[The University] simply has not carried its burden of demonstrating that it must prefer members of particular ethnic groups over all other individuals in order to promote better health-care delivery to deprived citizens. Indeed, [the University] has not shown that its preferential classification is likely to have any significant effect on the problem.

The fourth goal asserted by [the University] is the attainment of a diverse student body. This clearly is a constitutionally permissible goal for an institution of higher education. Academic freedom, though not a specifically enumerated constitutional right, long has been viewed as a special concern of the First Amendment. The freedom of a university to make its own judgments as to education includes the selection of its student body. Justice Frankfurter summarized the "four essential freedoms" that constitute academic freedom:

"'It is the business of a university to provide that atmosphere which is most conducive to speculation, experiment and creation. It is an atmosphere in which there prevail "the four essential freedoms" of a university - to determine for itself on academic grounds who may teach, what may be taught, how it shall be taught, and who may be admitted to study.'"

Our national commitment to the safeguarding of these freedoms within university communities was emphasized in *Keyishian v. Board of Regents* (1967):

"Our Nation is deeply committed to safeguarding academic freedom which is of transcendent value to all of us and not merely to the teachers concerned. That freedom is therefore a special concern of the First Amendment. . . . The Nation's future depends upon leaders trained through wide exposure to that robust exchange of ideas which discovers truth 'out of a multitude of tongues, [rather] than through any kind of authoritative selection.'"

The atmosphere of "speculation, experiment and creation" - so essential to the quality of higher education - is widely believed to be promoted by a diverse student body. As the Court noted in *Keyishian*, it is not too much to say that the "nation's future depends upon leaders trained through wide exposure" to the ideas and mores of students as diverse as this Nation of many peoples.

Thus, in arguing that its universities must be accorded the right to select those students who will contribute the most to the "robust exchange of ideas," [the University] invokes a countervailing constitutional interest, that of the First Amendment. In this light, [the University] must be viewed as seeking to achieve a goal that is of paramount importance in the fulfillment of its mission.

It may be argued that there is greater force to these views at the undergraduate level than in a medical school where the training is centered primarily on professional competency. But even at the graduate level, our tradition and experience lend support to the view that the contribution of diversity is substantial. In *Sweatt v. Painter*, the Court made a similar point with specific reference to legal education:

> "The law school, the proving ground for legal learning and practice, cannot be effective in isolation from the individuals and institutions with which the law interacts. Few students and no one who has practiced law would choose to study in an academic vacuum, removed from the interplay of ideas and the exchange of views with which the law is concerned."

Physicians serve a heterogeneous population. An otherwise qualified medical student with a particular background - whether it be ethnic, geographic, culturally advantaged or disadvantaged - may bring to a professional school of medicine experiences, outlooks, and ideas that enrich the training of its student body and better equip its graduates to render with understanding their vital service to humanity.

Ethnic diversity, however, is only one element in a range of factors a university properly may consider in attaining the goal of a heterogeneous student body. Although a university must have wide discretion in making the sensitive judgments as to who should be admitted, constitutional limitations protecting individual rights may not be disregarded. [Bakke] urges - and the courts below have held - that [the University]'s dual admissions program is a racial classification that impermissibly infringes his rights under the Fourteenth Amendment. As the interest of diversity is compelling in the context of a university's admissions program, the question remains whether the program's racial classification is necessary to promote this interest.

It may be assumed that the reservation of a specified number of seats in each class for individuals from the preferred ethnic groups would contribute to the attainment of considerable ethnic diversity in the student body. But [the University]'s argument that this is the only effective means of serving the interest of diversity is seriously flawed. In a most fundamental sense the argument misconceives the nature of the state interest that would justify consideration of race or ethnic background. It is not an interest in simple ethnic diversity, in which a specified percentage of the student body is in effect guaranteed to be members of selected ethnic groups, with the remaining percentage an undifferentiated aggregation of students. The diversity that furthers a compelling state interest encompasses a far broader array of qualifications and characteristics of which racial or ethnic origin is but a single though important element. [The University]'s special admissions program, focused *solely* on ethnic diversity, would hinder rather than further attainment of genuine diversity.

Nor would the state interest in genuine diversity be served by expanding [the University]'s two-track system into a multitrack program with a prescribed number of seats set aside for each identifiable category of applicants.

Indeed, it is inconceivable that a university would thus pursue the logic of [their] two-track program to the illogical end of insulating each category of applicants with certain desired qualifications from competition with all other applicants.

The experience of other university admissions programs, which take race into account in achieving the educational diversity valued by the First Amendment, demonstrates that the assignment of a fixed number of places to a minority group is not a necessary means toward that end. An illuminating example is found in the Harvard College program:

"In recent years Harvard College has expanded the concept of diversity to include students from disadvantaged economic, racial and ethnic groups. Harvard College now recruits not only Californians or Louisianans but also blacks and Chicanos and other minority students. . . .

"In practice, this new definition of diversity has meant that race has been a factor in some admission decisions. When the Committee on Admissions reviews the large middle group of applicants who are 'admissible' and deemed capable of doing good work in their courses, the race of an applicant may tip the balance in his favor just as geographic origin or a life spent on a farm may tip the balance in other candidates' cases. A farm boy from Idaho can bring something to Harvard College that a Bostonian cannot offer. Similarly, a black student can usually bring something that a white person cannot offer. . . .

"In Harvard College admissions the Committee
has not set target-quotas for the number of
blacks, or of musicians, football players, physi-
cists or Californians to be admitted in a given
year. . . . But that awareness [of the necessity of
including more than a token number of black stu-
dents] does not mean that the Committee sets a
minimum number of blacks or of people from
west of the Mississippi who are to be admitted. It
means only that in choosing among thousands of
applicants who are not only 'admissible' academi-
cally but have other strong qualities, the Committee, with a number of criteria in mind, pays some
attention to distribution among many types and
categories of students."

In such an admissions program, race or ethnic background
may be deemed a "plus" in a particular applicant's file, yet
it does not insulate the individual from comparison with
all other candidates for the available seats. The file of a
particular black applicant may be examined for his potential contribution to diversity without the factor of race
being decisive when compared, for example, with that of
an applicant identified as an Italian-American if the latter
is thought to exhibit qualities more likely to promote
beneficial educational pluralism. Such qualities could include exceptional personal talents, unique work or service
experience, leadership potential, maturity, demonstrated
compassion, a history of overcoming disadvantage, ability
to communicate with the poor, or other qualifications
deemed important. In short, an admissions program operated in this way is flexible enough to consider all perti-
nent elements of diversity in light of the particular qualifications of each applicant, and to place them on the same
footing for consideration, although not necessarily accord-

ing them the same weight. Indeed, the weight attributed to a particular quality may vary from year to year depending upon the "mix" both of the student body and the applicants for the incoming class.

This kind of program treats each applicant as an individual in the admissions process. The applicant who loses out on the last available seat to another candidate receiving a "plus" on the basis of ethnic background will not have been foreclosed from all consideration for that seat simply because he was not the right color or had the wrong surname. It would mean only that his combined qualifications, which may have included similar nonobjective factors, did not outweigh those of the other applicant. His qualifications would have been weighed fairly and competitively, and he would have no basis to complain of unequal treatment under the Fourteenth Amendment.

It has been suggested that an admissions program which considers race only as one factor is simply a subtle and more sophisticated - but no less effective - means of according racial preference than the Davis program. A facial intent to discriminate, however, is evident in [the University]'s preference program and not denied in this case. No such facial infirmity exists in an admissions program where race or ethnic background is simply one element - to be weighed fairly against other elements - in the selection process. "A boundary line," as Justice Frankfurter remarked in another connection, "is none the worse for being narrow." And a court would not assume that a university, professing to employ a facially nondiscriminatory admissions policy, would operate it as a cover for the functional equivalent of a quota system. In short, good faith would be presumed in the absence of a showing to the contrary in the manner permitted by our cases.

In summary, it is evident that the Davis special admissions program involves the use of an explicit racial classification never before countenanced by this Court. It tells applicants who are not Negro, Asian, or Chicano that they are totally excluded from a specific percentage of the seats in an entering class. No matter how strong their qualifications, quantitative and extracurricular, including their own potential for contribution to educational diversity, they are never afforded the chance to compete with applicants from the preferred groups for the special admissions seats. At the same time, the preferred applicants have the opportunity to compete for every seat in the class.

The fatal flaw in [the University]'s preferential program is its disregard of individual rights as guaranteed by the Fourteenth Amendment. Such rights are not absolute. But when a State's distribution of benefits or imposition of burdens hinges on ancestry or the color of a person's skin, that individual is entitled to a demonstration that the challenged classification is necessary to promote a substantial state interest. [The University] has failed to carry this burden. For this reason, that portion of the California court's judgment holding [the University of California]'s special admissions program invalid under the Fourteenth Amendment must be affirmed.

In enjoining [the University] from ever considering the race of any applicant, however, the courts below failed to recognize that the State has a substantial interest that legitimately may be served by a properly devised admissions program involving the competitive consideration of race and ethnic origin. For this reason, so much of the California court's judgment as enjoins [the University] from any consideration of the race of any applicant must be reversed.

With respect to [Bakke]'s entitlement to an injunction [a court order stopping an act] directing his admission to the Medical School, [the University] has conceded that it could not carry its burden of proving that, but for the existence of its unlawful special admissions program, [Bakke] still would not have been admitted. Hence, [Bakke] is entitled to the injunction, and that portion of the judgment must be affirmed.

THE U.S. CONSTITUTION

PREAMBLE

We the people of the United States, in order to form a more perfect union, establish justice, insure domestic tranquility, provide for the common defense, promote the general welfare, and secure the blessings of liberty to ourselves and our posterity, do ordain and establish this Constitution for the United States of America.

ARTICLE I

Section 1. All legislative powers herein granted shall be vested in a Congress of the United States, which shall consist of a Senate and House of Representatives.

Section 2. (1) The House of Representatives shall be composed of members chosen every second year by the people of several states, and the electors in each state shall have the qualifications requisite for electors of the most numerous branch of the State Legislature.

(2) No person shall be a Representative who shall not have attained to the age of twenty-five years, and been seven years a citizen of the United States, and who shall not, when elected, be an inhabitant of that state in which he shall be chosen.

(3) Representatives and direct taxes shall be apportioned among the several states which may be included within this union, according to their respective numbers, which shall be determined by adding to the whole number of free persons, including those bound to service for a term of years, and excluding Indians not taxed, three-fifths of all other persons. The actual enumeration shall be made

within three years after the first meeting of the Congress of the United States, and within every subsequent term of ten years, in such manner as they shall be law direct. The number of Representatives shall not exceed one for every thirty thousand, but each state shall have at least one Representative; and until such enumeration shall be made, the State of New Hampshire shall be entitled to choose three, Massachusetts eight, Rhode Island and Providence Plantations one, Connecticut five, New York six, New Jersey four, Pennsylvania eight, Delaware one, Maryland six, Virginia ten, North Carolina five, South Carolina five, and Georgia three.

(4) When vacancies happen in the representation from any state, the executive authority thereof shall issue Writs of Election to fill such vacancies.

(5) The House of Representatives shall choose their Speaker and other Officers; and shall have the sole power of impeachment.

Section 3. (1) The Senate of the United States shall be composed of two Senators from each state, chosen by the legislature thereof, for six years; and each Senator shall have one vote.

(2) Immediately after they shall be assembled in consequence of the first election, they shall be divided as equally as may be into three classes. The seats of the Senators of the first class shall be vacated at the expiration of the second year, of the second class at the expiration of the fourth year, and of the third class at the expiration of the sixth year, so that one-third may be chosen every second year; and if vacancies happen by resignation, or otherwise, during the recess of the legislature of any state, the execu-

tive thereof may take temporary appointments until the next meeting of the legislature, which shall then fill such vacancies.

(3) No person shall be a Senator who shall not have attained to the age of thirty years, and been nine years a citizen of the United States, and who shall not, when elected, be an inhabitant of that state for which he shall be chosen.

(4) The Vice President of the United States shall be President of the Senate, but shall have no vote, unless they be equally divided.

(5) The Senate shall choose their other Officers, and also a President pro tempore, in the absence of the Vice President, or when he shall exercise the Office of President of the United States.

(6) The Senate shall have the sole power to try all impeachments. When sitting for that purpose, they shall be on oath or affirmation. When the President of the United States is tried, the Chief Justice shall preside: and no person shall be convicted without the concurrence of two-thirds of the members present.

(7) Judgment in cases of impeachment shall not extend further than to removal from office, and disqualification to hold and enjoy any office of honor, trust, or profit under the United States: but the party convicted shall nevertheless be liable and subject to indictment, trial, judgment, and punishment, according to law.

Section 4. (1) The times, places and manner of holding elections for Senators and Representatives, shall be prescribed in each state by the legislature thereof; but the Congress may at any time by law make or alter such regulations, except as to the places of choosing Senators.

(2) The Congress shall assemble at least once in every year, and such meeting shall be on the first Monday in December, unless they shall by law appoint a different day.

Section 5. (1) Each House shall be the judge of the elections, returns, and qualifications of its own members, and a majority of each shall constitute a quorum to do business; but a smaller number may adjourn from day to day, and may be authorized to compel the attendance of absent members, in such manner, and under such penalties as each House may provide.

(2) Each House may determine the rules of its proceedings, punish its members for disorderly behavior, and, with the concurrence of two-thirds, expel a member.

(3) Each House shall keep a journal of its proceedings, and from time to time publish the same, excepting such parts as may in their judgment require secrecy; and the yeas and nays of the members of either House on any question shall, at the desire of one-fifth of those present, be entered on the journal.

(4) Neither House, during the Session of Congress, shall, without the consent of the other, adjourn for more than three days, nor to any other place than that in which the two Houses shall be sitting.

Section 6. (1) The Senators and Representatives shall receive a compensation for their services, to be ascertained by law, and paid out of the Treasury of the United States. They shall in all cases, except treason, felony and breach of the peace, be privileged from arrest during their attendance at the session of their respective Houses, and in going to and returning from the same; and for any speech or debate in either House, they shall not be questioned in any other place.

(2) No Senator or Representative shall, during the time for which he was elected, be appointed to any civil office under the authority of the United States, which shall have been created, or the emoluments whereof shall have been increased during such time and no person holding any office under the United States, shall be a member of either House during his continuance in office.

Section 7. (1) All bills for raising revenue shall originate in the House of Representatives; but the Senate may propose or concur with amendments as on other bills.

(2) Every bill which shall have passed the House of Representatives and the Senate, shall, before it become a law, be presented to the President of the United States; if he approve he shall sign it, but if not he shall return it, with his objections to the House in which it shall have originated, who shall enter the objections at large on their journal, and proceed to reconsider it. If after such reconsideration two-thirds of that House shall agree to pass the bill, it shall be sent together with the objections, to the other House, by which it shall likewise be reconsidered, and if approved by two-thirds of that House, it shall become a law. But in all such cases the votes of both Houses shall be determined by yeas and nays, and the names of the persons voting for and against the bill shall be entered on the journal of each House respectively. If any bill shall not

be returned by the President within ten days (Sundays excepted) after it shall have been presented to him, the same shall be a law, in like manner as if he had signed it, unless the Congress by their adjournment prevent its return in which case it shall not be a law.

(3) Every order,. resolution, of vote, to which the concurrence of the Senate and House of Representatives may be necessary (except on a question of adjournment) shall be presented to the President of the United States; and before the same shall take effect, shall be approved by him, or being disapproved by him, shall be repassed by two-thirds of the Senate and House of Representatives, according to the rules and limitations prescribed in the case of a bill.

Section 8. (1) The Congress shall have the power to lay and collect taxes, duties, imposts and excises, to pay the debts and provide for the common defense and general welfare of the United States; but all duties, imposts and excises shall be uniform throughout the United States;

(2) To borrow money on the credit of the United States;

(3) To regulate commerce with foreign nations, and among the several states, and with the Indian Tribes;

(4) To establish an uniform Rule of Naturalization, and uniform laws on the subject of bankruptcies throughout the United States;

(5) To coin money, regulate the value thereof, and of foreign coin, and fix the standard of weights and measures;

(6) To provide for the punishment of counterfeiting the securities and current coin of the United States;

(7) To establish Post Offices and Post Roads;

(8) To promote the progress of science and useful arts, by securing for limited times to authors and inventors the exclusive right to their respective writings and discoveries;

(9) To constitute tribunals inferior the Supreme Court;

(10) To define and punish piracies and felonies committed on the high seas, and offenses against the Law of Nations;

(11) To declare war, grant Letters of Marque and Reprisal, and make rules concerning captures on land and water;

(12) To raise and support armies, but no appropriation of money to that use shall be for a longer term than two years;

(13) To provide and maintain a Navy;

(14) To make rules for the government and regulation of the land and naval forces;

(15) To provide for calling forth the Militia to execute the laws of the Union, suppress insurrections and repel invasions;

(16) To provide for organizing, arming, and disciplining, the Militia, and for governing such part of them as may be employed in the service of the United States, reserving to the states respectively, the appointment of the Officers,

and the authority of training the Militia according to the discipline prescribed by Congress;

(17) To exercise exclusive legislation in all cases whatsoever, over such district (not exceeding ten miles square) as may, be cession of particular states, and the acceptance of Congress, become the Seat of the Government of the United States, and to exercise like authority over all places purchased by the consent of the legislature of the state in which the same shall be, for the erection of forts, magazines, arsenals, dockyards, and other needful buildings; -- and

(18) To make all laws which shall be necessary and proper for carrying into execution the foregoing powers, and all other powers vested by this Constitution in the Government of the United States, or in any Department or Officer thereof.

Section 9. (1) The migration or importation of such persons as any of the states now existing shall think proper to admit, shall not be prohibited by the Congress prior to the year one thousand eight hundred and eight, but a tax or duty may be imposed on such importation, not exceeding ten dollars for each person.

(2) The privilege of the Writ of Habeas Corpus shall not be suspended, unless when in cases of rebellion or invasion the public safety may require it.

(3) No Bill of Attainder or ex post facto law shall be passed.

(4) No capitation, or other direct, tax shall be laid, unless in proportion to the Census or enumeration herein before directed to be taken.

(5) No tax or duty shall be laid on articles exported from any state.

(6) No preference shall be given by any regulation of commerce or revenue to th ports of one state over those of another: nor shall vessels bound to, or from, one state be obliged to enter, clear, or pay duties in another.

(7) No money shall be drawn from the Treasury, but in consequence eof appropriations made by law; and a regular statement and account of the receipts and expenditures of all public money shall be published from time to time.

(8) No title of nobility shall be granted by the United States: and no person holding any office of profit or trust under them, shall, without the consent of the Congress, accept of any present, emolument, office, or title, of any kind whatever, from any King, Prince, or foreign State.

Section 10. (1) No state shall enter into any treaty, alliance, or confederation; grant Letter of Marque and Reprisal; coin money; emit bills of credit; make any thing but gold and silver coin a tender in payment of debts; pass and Bill of Attainder, ex post facto law, or law impairing the obligation of contracts, or grant any title of nobility.

(2) No state shall, without the consent of the Congress, lay any imposts or duties on imports or exports, except what may be absolutely necessary for executing its inspection laws: and the net produce of all duties and imposts, laid by any state on imports or exports, shall be for the use of

the Treasury of the United States; and all such laws shall
be subject to the revision and control of the Congress.

(3) No state shall, without the consent of Congress, lay
any duty of tonnage, keep troops, or ships of war in time
of peace, enter into any agreement or compact with another state, or with a foreign power, or engage in war, unless
actually invaded, or in such imminent danger as will not
admit of delay.

ARTICLE II

Section 1. (1) The executive power shall be vested in a
President of the United States of America. He shall hold
his office during the term of four years, and, together
with the Vice President, chosen for the same term, be
elected, as follows:

(2) Each state shall appoint, in such manner as the legislature thereof may direct, a number of electors, equal to the
whole number of Senators and Representatives to which
the state may be entitled in the Congress; but no Senator
or Representative, or person holding an office of trust or
profit under the United States, shall be appointed an Elector.

(3) The Electors shall meet in their respective states, and
vote by ballot for two persons, of whom one at least shall
not be an inhabitant of the same state with themselves.
And they shall make a list of all the persons voted for,
and of the number of votes for each; which list they shall
sign and certify, and transmit sealed to the Seat of the
Government of the United States, directed to the President of the Senate. The President of the Senate shall, in
the presence of the Senate and House of Representatives,

open all the certificates, and the votes shall then be counted. The person having the greatest number of votes shall be the President, if such number be a majority of the whole number of Electors appointed; and if there be more than one who have such majority, and have an equal number of votes, then the House of Representatives shall immediately choose by ballot one of them for President; and if no person have a majority, then from the five highest on the list the said House shall in like manner choose the President. But in choosing the President, the votes shall be taken by states the representation from each state having one vote; a quorum for this purpose shall consist of a member or members from two-thirds of the states, and a majority of all the states shall be necessary to a choice. In every case, after the choice of the President, the person having the greater number of votes of the Electors shall be the Vice President. But if there should remain two or more who have equal votes, the Senate shall choose from them by ballot the Vice President.

(4) The Congress may determine the time of choosing the Electors, and the day on which they shall give their votes; which day shall be the same throughout the United States.

(5) No person except a natural born citizen, or a citizen of the United States, at the time of the adoption of this Constitution, shall be eligible to the Office of President; neither shall any person be eligible to that Office who shall not have attained to the age of thirty-five years, and been fourteen years a resident within the United States.

(6) In case of the removal of the President from Office, or of his death, resignation or inability to discharge the powers and duties of the said Office, the same shall devolve on the Vice President, and the Congress may by law

provide for the case of removal, death, resignation of inability, both of the President and Vice President, declaring
what Officer shall then act as President, and such Officer
shall act accordingly, until the disability be removed, or a
President shall be elected.

(7) The President shall, at stated times, receive for his
services, a compensation, which shall neither be increased
nor diminished during the period for which he shall have
been elected, and he shall not receive within that period
any other emolument from the United States, or any of
them.

(8) Before he enter on the execution of his Office, he
shall take the following Oath or Affirmation: "I do solemnly swear (or affirm) that I will faithfully execute the
Office of President of the United States, and will to the
best of my ability, preserve, protect and defend the Constitution of the United States."

Section 2. (1) The President shall be Commander in Chief
of the Army and Navy of the United States, and of the
militia of the several states, when called into the actual
service of the United States; he may require the opinion,
in writing, of the principal Officer in each of the Executive Departments, upon any subject relating to the duties
of their respective Offices, and he shall have power to
grant reprieves and pardons for offenses against the United States, except in cases of impeachment.

(2) He shall have power, by and with the advice and consent of the Senate to make treaties, provided two-thirds of
the Senators present concur; and he shall nominate, and
by and with the advice and consent of the Senate, shall appoint Ambassadors, other public Ministers and Consuls,

Judges of the supreme Court, and all other Officers of the
United States, whose appointments are not herein otherwise provided for, and which shall be established by law;
but the Congress may be law vest the appointment of such
inferior Officers, as they think proper, in the President
alone, in the courts of law, or in the Heads of Departments.

(3) The President shall have power to fill up all vacancies
that may happen during the recess of the Senate, by granting commissions which shall expire at the end of their
next Session.

Section 3. He shall from time to time give to the Congress
information of the State of the Union, and recommend to
their consideration such measures as he shall judge necessary and expedient; he may, on extraordinary occasions,
convene both Houses, or either of them, and in case of disagreement between them, with respect to the time of adjournment, he may adjourn them to such time as he shall
think proper; he shall receive Ambassadors and other public Ministers; he shall take care that the laws be faithfully
executed, and shall commission all the Officers of the
United States.

Section 4. The President, Vice President and all civil Officers of the United States, shall be removed from office on
impeachment for, and conviction of, treason, bribery, or
other high crimes and misdemeanors.

ARTICLE III

Section 1. The judicial power of the United States, shall
be vested in one supreme Court, and in such inferior
courts as the Congress may from time to time ordain and

establish. The Judges, both of the supreme and inferior courts, shall hold their Offices during good behaviour, and shall, at stated times, receive for their services a compensation, which shall not be diminished during their continuance in office.

Section 2. (1) The judicial power shall extend to all cases, in law and equity, arising under this Constitution, the laws of the United States, and treaties made, or which shall be made, under their authority; -- to all cases affecting Ambassadors, other public Ministers and Consuls; -- to all cases of admiralty and maritime jurisdiction; -- to controversies to which the United States shall be a party; -- to controversies between two or more states; -- between a state and citizens of another state; -- between citizens of different states; -- between citizens of the same state claiming lands under the grants of different states, and between a state, or the citizens thereof, and foreign states, citizens or subjects.

(2) In all cases affecting Ambassadors, other public Ministers and Consuls, and those in which a state shall be a party, the supreme Court shall have original jurisdiction. In all the other cases before mentioned, the supreme Court shall have appellate jurisdiction, both as to law and fact, with such exceptions, and under such regulations as the Congress shall make.

(3) The trial of all crimes, except in cases of impeachment, shall be by jury; and such trial shall be held in the state where the said crimes shall have been committed; but when not committed within any state, the trial shall be at such place or places as the Congress may be law have directed.

Section 3. (1) Treason against the United States, shall consist only in levying war against them, or, in adhering to their enemies, giving them aid and comfort. No person shall be convicted of treason unless on the testimony of two witnesses to the same overt act, or on confession in open Court.

(2) The Congress shall have power to declare the punishment of treason, but no Attainder of Treason shall work corruption of blood, or forfeiture except during the life of the person attainted.

ARTICLE IV

Section 1. Full faith and credit shall be given in each state to the public acts, records, and judicial proceedings of every other state. And the Congress may by general laws prescribe the manner in which such acts, records and proceedings shall be proved, and the effect thereof.

Section 2. (1) The citizens of each state shall be entitled to all privileges and immunities of citizens in the several states.

(2) A person charged in any state with treason, felony, or other crime, who shall flee from justice, and be found in another state, shall on demand of the executive authority of the state from which he fled, be delivered up, to be removed to the state having jurisdiction of the crime.

(3) No person held to service or labour in one state, under the laws thereof, escaping into another, shall, in consequence of any law or regulation therein, be discharged from such service or labour, but shall be delivered up on

claim of the party to whom such service or labour may be due.

Section 3. (1) New states may be admitted by the Congress into this Union; but no new state shall be formed or erected within the jurisdiction of any other state; nor any state be formed by the junction of two or more states, or parts of states, without the consent of the legislatures of the states concerned as well as of the Congress.

(2) The Congress shall have power to dispose of and make all needful rules and regulations respecting the territory or other property belonging to the United States; and nothing in this Constitution shall be so construed as to prejudice any claims of the United States, or of any particular state.

Section 4. The United States shall guarantee to every state in this Union a Republican form of government, and shall protect each of them against invasion; and on application of the Legislature, or of the Executive (when the Legislature cannot be convened) against domestic violence.

ARTICLE V

The Congress, whenever two-thirds of both Houses shall deem it necessary, shall propose amendments to this Constitution, or, on the application of the Legislatures of two-thirds of the several states, shall call a convention for proposing amendments, which, in either case, shall be valid to all intents and purposes, as part of this constitution, when ratified by the Legislatures of three-fourths of the several states, or by conventions in three-fourths thereof, as the one or the other mode of ratification may be proposed by the Congress; provided that no amendment which may be made prior to the year one thousand eight hundred and eight shall in any manner affect the first and fourth clauses in the Ninth Section of the first Article; and that no state, without its consent, shall be deprived of its equal suffrage in the Senate.

ARTICLE VI

(1) All debts contracted and engagements entered into, before the adoption of this Constitution shall be as valid against the United States under this Constitution, as under the Confederation.

(2) This Constitution, and the laws of the United States which shall be made in pursuance thereof; and all treaties made, or which shall be made, under the authority of the United States, shall be the supreme law of the land; and the Judges in every state shall be bound thereby, any thing in the Constitution or laws of any state to the contrary notwithstanding.

(3) The Senators and Representatives before mentioned, and the Members of the several State Legislatures, and all executive and judicial Officers, both of the United States and of the several states, shall be bound by oath or affirmation, to support this Constitution; but no religious test shall ever be required as a qualification to any Office or public trust under the United States.

ARTICLE VII

The ratification of the Conventions of nine states shall be sufficient for the establishment of this Constitution between the states so ratifying the same.

AMENDMENT I (1791)

Congress shall make no law respecting an establishment of religion, or prohibiting the free exercise thereof; or abridging the freedom of speech, or of the press; or the right of the people peaceably to assemble, and to petition the Government for a redress of grievances.

AMENDMENT II (1791)

A well regulated Militia, being necessary to the security of a free State, the right of the people to keep and bear arms, shall not be infringed.

AMENDMENT III (1791)

No soldier shall, in time of peace be quartered in any house, without the consent of the owner, nor in time of war, but in a manner to be prescribed by law.

AMENDMENT IV (1791)

The right of the people to be secure in their persons, houses, papers, and effects, against unreasonable searches and seizures, shall not be violated, and no warrants shall issue, but upon probable cause, supported by oath or affirmation, and particularly describing the place to be searched, and the persons or things to be seized.

AMENDMENT V (1791)

No person shall be held to answer for a capital, or otherwise infamous crime, unless on a presentment or indictment of a Grand Jury, except in cases arising in the land or naval forces, or in the Militia, when in actual service in time of war or public danger; nor shall any person be subject for the same offense to be twice put in jeopardy of life or limb; nor shall be compelled in any criminal case to be a witness against himself, nor be deprived of life, liberty, or property, without due process of law; nor shall private property be taken for public use, without just compensation.

AMENDMENT VI (1791)

In all criminal prosecutions, the accused shall enjoy the right to a speedy and public trial, by an impartial jury of the state and district wherein the crime shall have been committed, which district shall have been previously ascertained by law, and to be informed of the nature and cause of the accusation; to be confronted with the witnesses against him; to have compulsory process for obtaining witnesses in his favor, and to have the assistance of counsel for his defense.

AMENDMENT VII (1791)

In suits at common law, where the value in controversy shall exceed twenty dollars, the right of trial by jury shall be preserved, and no fact tried by jury, shall be otherwise re-examined in any Court of the United States, than according to the rules of the common law.

AMENDMENT VIII (1791)

Excessive bail shall not be required, nor excessive fines imposed, nor cruel and unusual punishments inflicted.

AMENDMENT IX (1791)

The enumeration in the Constitution, of certain rights, shall not be construed to deny or disparage others retained by the people.

AMENDMENT X (1791)

The powers not delegated to the United States by the Constitution, nor prohibited by it to the States, are reserved to the States respectively, or to the people.

AMENDMENT XI (1798)

The judicial power of the United States shall not be construed to extend to any suit in law or equity, commenced or prosecuted against one of the United States by citizens of another state, or by citizens or subjects of any foreign state.

AMENDMENT XII (1804)

The Electors shall meet in their respective states and vote by ballot for President and Vice-President, one of whom, at least, shall not be an inhabitant of the same stat with themselves; they shall name in their ballots the person voted for as President, and in distinct ballots the person voted for as Vice-President, and they shall make distinct lists of all persons voted for as President, and of all persons voted for as Vice-President, and of the number of votes for each, which lists they shall sign and certify, and transmit sealed to the seat of the government of the United States, directed to the President of the Senate; -- the President of the Senate shall, in the presence of the Senate and House of Representatives, open all the certificates and the votes shall then be counted; -- the person having the greatest number of votes for President, shall be the President, if such number be a majority of the persons having the highest numbers not exceeding three on the list of those voted for as President, the House of Representatives shall choose immediately, by ballot, the President. But in choosing the President, the votes shall be taken by states, the representation from each state having one vote; a quorum for his purpose shall consist of a member or members from two-thirds of the states, and a majority of all the states shall be necessary to a choice. And if the House of Representatives shall not choose a President whenever the right of choice shall devolve upon them before the fourth day of March next following, then the Vice-President shall act as President, as in the case of the death or other constitutional disability of the President. -- The person having the greatest number of votes as Vice-President, shall be the Vice-President, if such number be a majority of the whole number of Electors appointed, and if no person have a majority, then from the two highest numbers on the list, the Senate shall choose the Vice-President; a quorum for the purpose shall consist of two-thirds of the whole number of Senators, and a majority of the whole number shall be necessary to a choice. But no person constitutionally ineligible to the office of President shall be eligible to that of Vice-President of the United States.

AMENDMENT XIII (1865)

Section 1. Neither slavery nor involuntary servitude, except as a punishment for crime whereof the party shall have been duly convicted, shall exist within the United States, or any place subject to their jurisdiction.

Section 2. Congress shall have power to enforce this article by appropriate legislation.

AMENDMENT XIV (1868)

Section 1. All persons born or naturalized in the United States, and subject to the jurisdiction thereof, are citizens of the United States and of the state wherein they reside. No state shall make or enforce any law which shall abridge the privileges or immunities of citizens of the United States; nor shall any state deprive any person of life, liberty, or property, without due process of law; nor deny to any person within its jurisdiction the equal protection of the laws.

Section 2. Representatives shall be apportioned among the several states according to their respective numbers, counting the whole number of persons in each State excluding Indians not taxed. But when the right to vote at any election for the choice of electors for President and Vice President of the United States, Representatives in Congress, the Executive and Judicial officers of a state, or the members of the Legislature thereof, is denied to any of the male inhabitants of such state, being twenty-one years of age, and citizens of the United States, or in any way abridged, except for participation in rebellion, or other crime, the basis of representation therein shall be reduced in the proportion which the number of such male citizens shall bear to the whole number of male citizens twenty-one years of age in such state.

Section 3. No person shall be a Senator or Representative in Congress, or elector of President and Vice President, or hold any office, civil or military, under the United States, or under any state, who having previously taken an oath, as a member of Congress, or as an officer of the United States, or as a member of any state legislature, or as an executive or judicial officer of any state, to support the Constitution of the United States, shall have engaged in insurrection or rebellion against the same, or given aid or comfort to the enemies thereof. But Congress may by a vote of two-thirds of each House, remove such disability.

Section 4. The validity of the public debt of the United States, authorized by law, including debts incurred for payment of pensions and bounties for services in suppressing insurrection or rebellion, shall not be questioned. But neither the United States nor any state shall assume or pay any debt or obligation incurred in aid of insurrection or rebellion against the United States, or any claim for the loss or emancipation of any slave; but all such debts, obligations and claims shall be held illegal and void.

Section 5. The Congress shall have power to enforce, by appropriate legislation, the provisions of this article.

AMENDMENT XV (1870)

Section 1. The right of citizens of the United States to vote shall not be denied or abridged by the United States or by any state on account of race, color, or previous condition of servitude.

Section 2. The Congress shall have power to enforce this article by appropriate legislation.

AMENDMENT XVI (1913)

The Congress shall have power to lay and collect taxes on income, from whatever source derived, without apportionment among the several states, and without regard to any census or enumeration.

AMENDMENT XVII (1913)

(1) The Senate of the United States shall be composed of two Senators from each state, elected by the people thereof, for six years; and each Senator shall have one vote. The electors in each State shall have the qualifications requisite for electors of the most numerous branch of the state legislatures.

(2) When vacancies happen in the representation of any state in the Senate, the executive authority of such state shall issue writs of election to fill such vacancies: *provided,* that the legislature of any state may empower the executive thereof to make temporary appointments until the people fill the vacancies by election as the legislature may direct.

(3) This amendment shall not be so construed as to affect the election or term of any Senator chosen before it becomes valid as part of the Constitution.

AMENDMENT XVIII (1919)

Section 1. After one year from the ratification of this article the manufacture, sale, or transportation of intoxicating liquors within, the importation thereof into, or the exportation thereof from the United States and all territory subject to the jurisdiction thereof for beverage purposes is hereby prohibited.

Section 2. The Congress and the several states shall have concurrent power to enforce this article by appropriate legislation.

Section 3. This article shall be inoperative unless it shall have been ratified as an amendment to the Constitution by the legislatures of the several states, as provided in the Constitution, within seven years from the date of the submission hereof to the states by the Congress.

AMENDMENT XIX (1920)

(1) The right of citizens of the United States to vote shall not be denied or abridged by the United States or by any state on account of sex.

(2) Congress shall have power to enforce this article by appropriate legislation.

AMENDMENT XX (1933)

Section 1. The terms of the President and Vice President shall end at noon on the 20th day of January, and the terms of Senators and Representatives at noon on the 3d day of January, of the years in which such terms would have ended if this article had not been ratified; and the terms of their successors shall then begin.

Section 2. The Congress shall assemble at least once in every year, and such meeting shall begin at noon on the 3d day of January, unless they shall by law appoint a different day.

Section 3. If, at the time fixed for the beginning of the term of the President, the President elect shall have died,

the Vice President elect shall become President. If the
President shall not have been chosen before the time fixed for the beginning of his term, or if the President elect
shall have failed to qualify, then the Vice President elect
shall act as President until a President shall have qualified; and the Congress may by law provide for the case
wherein neither a President elect nor a Vice President
elect shall have qualified, declaring who shall then act as
President, or the manner in which one who is to act shall
be selected, and such person shall act accordingly until a
President or Vice President shall have qualified.

Section 4. The Congress may by law provide for the case
of the death of any of the persons from whom the House
of Representatives may choose a President whenever the
right of choice shall have devolved upon them, and for
the case of the death of any of the persons from whom
the Senate may choose a Vice President whenever the
right of choice shall have devolved upon them.

Section 5. Sections 1 and 2 shall take effect on the 15th
day of October following the ratification of this article.

Section 6. This article shall be inoperative unless it shall
have been ratified as an amendment to the Constitution
by the legislatures of three-fourths of the several states
within seven years from the date of its submission.

AMENDMENT XXI (1933)

Section 1. The eighteenth article of amendment to the
Constitution of the United States is hereby repealed.

Section 2. The transportation or importation into any
state, territory, or possession of the United States for de-

livery or use therein of intoxicating liquors, in violation of the laws thereof, is hereby prohibited.

Section 3. This article shall be inoperative unless it shall have been ratified as an amendment to the Constitution by conventions in the several states, as provided in the Constitution, within seven years from the date of the submission hereof to the states by the Congress.

AMENDMENT XXII (1951)

Section 1. No person shall be elected to the office of the President more than twice, and no person who has held the office of President, or acted as President, for more than two ears of a term to which some other person was elected President shall be elected to the office of President more than once. But this Article shall not apply to any person holding the office of President when this Article was proposed by the Congress, and shall not prevent any person who may be holding the office of President, or acting as President, during the term within which this Article becomes operative from holding the office of President or acting as President during the remainder of such term.

Section 2. This article shall be inoperative unless it shall have been ratified as an amendment to the Constitution by the legislatures of three-fourths of the several states within seven years from the date of its submission to the states by the Congress.

AMENDMENT XXIII (1961)

Section 1. The District constituting the seat of Government of the United States shall appoint in such manner as the Congress may direct:

A number of electors of President and Vice President equal to the whole number of Senators and Representatives in Congress to which the District would be entitled if it were a state, but in no event more than the least populous state; they shall be in addition to those appointed by the states, but they shall be considered, for the purposes of the election of President and Vice President, to be electors appointed by a state; and they shall meet in the District and perform such duties as provided by the twelfth article of amendment.

Section 2. The Congress shall have power to enforce this article by appropriate legislation.

AMENDMENT XXIV (1964)

Section 1. The right of citizens of the United States to vote in any primary or other election for President or Vice President, for electors for President or Vice President, or for Senator or Representative in Congress, shall not be denied or abridged by the United States, or any state by reason of failure to pay any poll tax or other tax.

Section 2. The Congress shall have power to enforce this article by appropriate legislation.

AMENDMENT XXV (1967)

Section 1. In case of the removal of the President from office or of his death or resignation, the Vice President shall become President.

Section 2. Whenever there is a vacancy in the office of the Vice President, the President shall nominate a Vice President who shall take office upon confirmation by a majority vote of both Houses of Congress.

Section 3. Whenever the President transmits to the President pro tempore of the Senate and the Speaker of the House of Representatives his written declaration that he is unable to discharge the powers and duties of his office, and until he transmits to them a written declaration to the contrary, such powers and duties shall be discharged by the Vice President as Acting President.

Section 4. Whenever the Vice President and a majority of either the principal officers of the executive departments or of such other body as Congress may by law provide, transmit to the President pro tempore of the Senate and the Speaker of the House of Representatives their written declaration that the President is unable to discharge the powers and duties of his office, the Vice President shall immediately assume the powers and duties of the office as Acting President.

Thereafter, when the President transmits to the President pro tempore of the Senate and the Speaker of the House of Representatives his written declaration that no inability exists, he shall resume the powers and duties of his office unless the Vice President and a majority of either the principal officers of the executive department or of such other body as Congress may by law provide, transmit within four days to the President pro tempore of the Senate and the Speaker of the House of Representatives their written declaration and the President is unable to discharge the powers and duties of his office. Thereupon Congress shall decide the issue, assembling within forty-eight hours for that purpose if not in session. If the Congress, within twenty-one days after receipt of the latter written declaration, or, if Congress is not in session, within twenty-one days after Congress is required to assemble, determines by two-thirds vote of both Houses that the President is unable to discharge the power and duties of his office, the Vice President shall continue to discharge the same as Acting President; otherwise, the President shall resume the powers and duties of his office.

AMENDMENT XXVI (1971)

Section 1. The right of citizens of the United States, who are eighteen years of age or older, to vote shall not be denied or abridged by the United States or by any state on account of age.

Section 2. The Congress shall have power to enforce this article by appropriate legislation.

AMENDMENT XXVII (1992)

No law, varying the compensation for the services of the Senators and Representatives, shall take effect, until an election of Representatives shall have intervened.

BIBLIOGRAPHY

THE JAPANESE AMERICAN DECISIONS

Daniels, Roger, *Concentration Camps: North American Japanese in the United States and Canada During World War II*, Melbourne: Krieger Publishing Co., 1981.

Grodzins, Morton, *Americans Betrayed: Politics and the Japanese Evacuation*, Chicago: University of Chicago Press, 1949.

Houston, Jeanne Wakatsuki and James D. Houston, *Farewell to Manzaner: A True Story of Japanese American Experience During and After the World War II Internment*, Boston, MA: Houghton-Mifflin, 1973.

Irons, Peter, Editor, *Justice Delayed: The Record of the Japanese American Internment Cases*, Middleton, CT: Wesleyan University Press, 1989.

Rostow, Eugene V., *The Japanese American Cases - A Disaster*, New Haven, CT: Yale Law Journal 54: 489-533 (1989).

Taylor, Sandra C., *Jewel of the Desert: Japanese American Internment at Topaz*, Berkeley, CA: University of California Press, 1993.

THE AFRICAN AMERICAN DECISIONS

MOB JUSTICE

Carter, Dan T., *Scottsboro: A Tragedy of the American South*, Baton Rouge, LA: Louisiana State University Press, 1969.

Chalmers, Allan Knight, *They Shall Be Free*, Garden City, NY: Doubleday, 1951.

Covin, Kelly, *Hear That Train Blow: A Novel About the Scottsboro Case*, New York, NY: Delacorte Press, 1970.

Norris, Clarence and Sybil D. Washington, *The Last of the Scottsboro Boys: An Autobiography*, New York, NY: Putnam, 1979.

Patterson, Haywood, and Earl Conrad, *Scottsboro Boy*, Garden City, NY: Doubleday, 1950.

Williams, Lee E. and Lee E. Williams II, *Anatomy of Four Race Riots: Racial Conflict in Knoxville, Elaine, Tulsa and Chicago, 1919-1921*, Hattiesburg, MS: University and College Press of Mississippi, 1972.

SCHOOL DESEGREGATION

Blaustein, Albert P. and Clarence C. Ferguson, Jr., *Desegregation and the Law: The Meaning of the School Segregation Cases*, New Brunswick, NJ: Rutgers University Press, 1957.

Orfield, Gary, *Must We Bus? Segregated Schools and National Policy*, Washington, DC: Brookings Institution, 1978.

Schwartz, Bernard, *Swann's Way: The School Busing Case and the Supreme Court*, New York, NY: Oxford University Press, 1986.

United States Commission on Civil Rights, *School Desegregation in Little Rock, Arkansas*, Washington, DC: The Commission, 1977.

Wolters, Raymond, *The Burden of Brown: Thirty Years of School Desegregation*, Knoxville, TN: The University of Tennessee Press, 1984.

THE RIGHT TO VOTE

Finkelman, Paul, Editor, *African-Americans and the Right to Vote*, New York, NY: Garland, 1992.

National Urban League, *Abridging the Right to Vote*, New York, NY: National Urban League, 1972.

PUBLIC TRANSPORTATION

Armstrong, Nancy, *The Study of an Attempt Made in 1943 to Abolish Segregation of the Races on Common Carriers in the State of Virginia*, Charlottesville, VA: University of Virginia, 1950.

Barnes, Catherine A., *Journey from Jim Crow: The Desegregation of Southern Transit*, New York, NY: Columbia University Press, 1983.

RACIALLY RESTRICTED HOUSING

Graham, Jamie R., *Shelley v. Kraemer: A Celebration*, St. Louis, MO: Girl Friends, Inc., 1988.

Long, Herman H. and Charles S. Johnson, *People vs. Property: Race Restrictive Covenants in Housing*, Nashville, TN: Fiske University Press, 1947.

PUBLIC ACCOMMODATIONS

Carothers, Leslie A., *The Public Accommodations Law of 1964: Arguments, Issues and Attitudes in a Legal Debate*, Northampton, MA: Smith College, 1968.

The Drive to Desegregation: Places of Public Accommodation, New York, NY: Garland Press, 1991.

INTERRACIAL MARRIAGE

Cretser, Gary A., and Joseph J. Leon, Editors, *Intermarriage in the United States*, Binghamton, NY: Haworth Press, 1982.

Huber, Patrick, *Two Races Beyond the Altar*, Boston, MA: Branden Publishing Company, 1976.

Sickels, Robert J., *Race, Marriage and the Law*, Albuquerque, NM: University of New Mexico Press, 1972.

Sohn, Chang Moon, *Principle and Expediency in Judicial Review: Miscegenation Cases in the Supreme Court*, Ann Arbor, MI: UMI, 1971.

AFFIRMATIVE ACTION

O'Neill, Timothy J., *Bakke and the Politics of Equality*, Middletown, CT: Wesleyan University Press, 1985.

Schwartz, Bernard, *Behind Bakke: Affirmative Action and the Supreme Court*, New York, NY: New York University Press, 1988.

Woods, Geraldine, *Affirmative Action*, New York, NY: Impact Books, 1989.

THE SUPREME COURT

Abraham, Henry Julian, *Freedom and the Court: Civil Rights and Liberties in the United States*, New York, NY: Oxford University Press, 1967.

Agresto, John, *The Supreme Court and Constitutional Democracy*, Ithaca, NY: Cornell University Press, 1984.

Braeman, John, *Before the Civil Rights Revolution: The Old Court and Individual Rights*, New York, NY: Green wood Press, 1988.

Cox, Archibald, *The Court and the Constitution*, New York, NY: Houghton-Mifflin, 1988.

Dumbauld, Edward, *The Bill of Rights and What It Means Today*, New York, NY: Greenwood Press, 1979.

Ginger, Ann Fagan, *The Law, The Supreme Court, and The People's Rights*, Woodbury, NY: Barron's Educa tional Series, 1973.

Goode, Stephen, *The Controversial Court: Supreme Court Influences on American Life*, New York, NY: Messner, 1982.

Kairys, David, *With Liberty and Justice for Some*, New York, NY: The New Press, 1993.

Lawson, Don, *Landmark Supreme Court Cases*, Hillside: Enslow Publishers, Inc., 1987.

Rehnquist, William H., *The Supreme Court: How It Was, How It Is*, New York, NY: Morrow, 1987.

Woodward, Bob, and Scott Armstrong, *The Brethren: Inside the Supreme Court*, New York, NY: Simon & Schuster, 1979.

Index

EXCELLENT BOOKS ORDER FORM

(Please xerox this form so it will be available to other readers.)

Please send

Copy(ies)

_____ of CIVIL RIGHTS DECISIONS: 19th CENTURY @ $16.95 ea.

_____ of CIVIL RIGHTS DECISIONS: 20th CENTURY @ $16.95 ea.

_____ of ABRAHAM LINCOLN: WORD FOR WORD @ $19.95 each

_____ of THOMAS JEFFERSON: WORD FOR WORD @ $19.95 each

_____ of JOHN F. KENNEDY: WORD FOR WORD @ $19.95 each

_____ of LANDMARK DECISIONS @ $14.95 each

_____ of LANDMARK DECISIONS II @ $15.95 each

_____ of LANDMARK DECISIONS III @ $15.95 each

_____ of LANDMARK DECISIONS IV @ $15.95 each

_____ of THE ADA HANDBOOK @ $15.95 each

_____ of ABORTION DECISIONS: THE 1970's @ $15.95 each

_____ of ABORTION DECISIONS: THE 1980's @ $15.95 each

_____ of ABORTION DECISIONS: THE 1990's @ $15.95 each

Name: _____

Address: _____

City: _____ **State:** _____ **Zip:** _____

Add $1 per book for shipping and handling
California residents add sales tax

OUR GUARANTEE: Any Excellent Book may be returned at any time for any reason and a full refund will be made.

Mail your check or money order to: Excellent Books, Post Office Box 927105, San Diego, California 92192-7105 or call (619) 457-4895